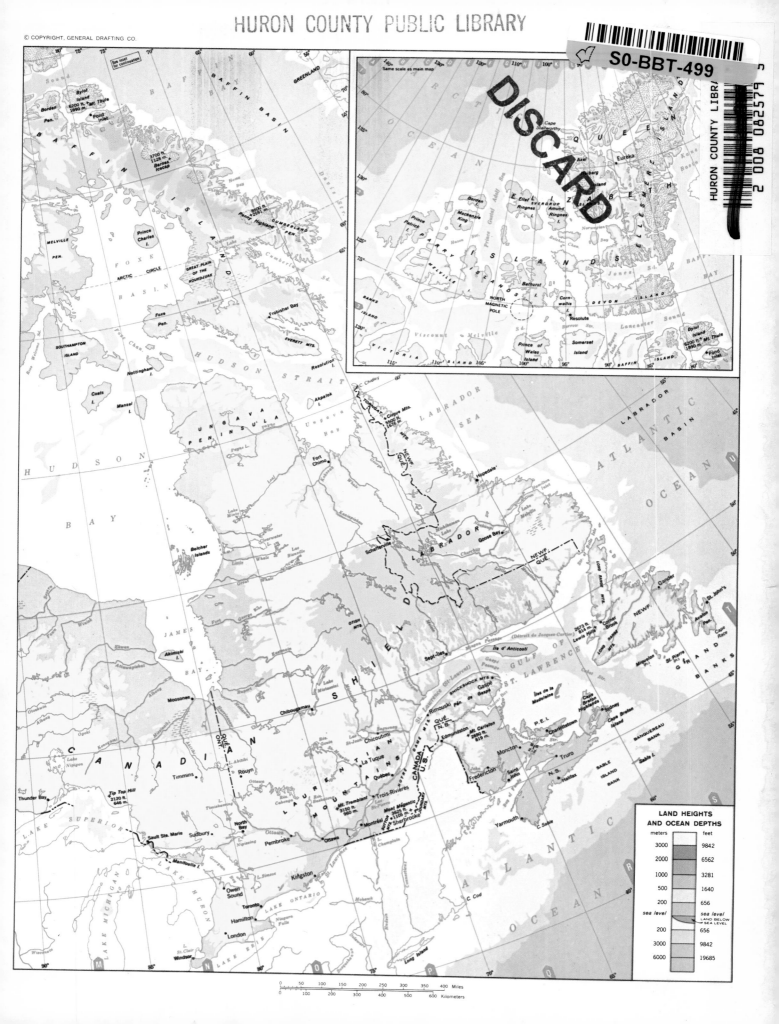

LAND HEIGHTS
AND OCEAN DEPTHS

meters		feet
3000		9842
2000		6562
1000		3281
500		1640
200		656
sea level		sea level
		LAND BELOW SEA LEVEL
200		656
3000		9842
6000		19685

0 50 100 150 200 250 300 350 400 Miles
0 100 200 300 400 500 600 Kilometers

Canada

ANTHONY HOCKING

Publisher: John Rae

Managing Editor: Robin Brass

Manuscript Editor: Jocelyn Van Huyse

Production Supervisor: Lynda Rhodes

Graphics: Pirjo Selistemagi

Cover: Brian F. Reynolds

THE CANADA SERIES

McGRAW-HILL RYERSON LIMITED

Toronto Montreal New York St. Louis San Francisco
Auckland Bogotá Guatemala Hamburg Johannesburg
Lisbon London Madrid Mexico New Delhi Panama
Paris San Juan São Paulo Singapore Sydney Tokyo

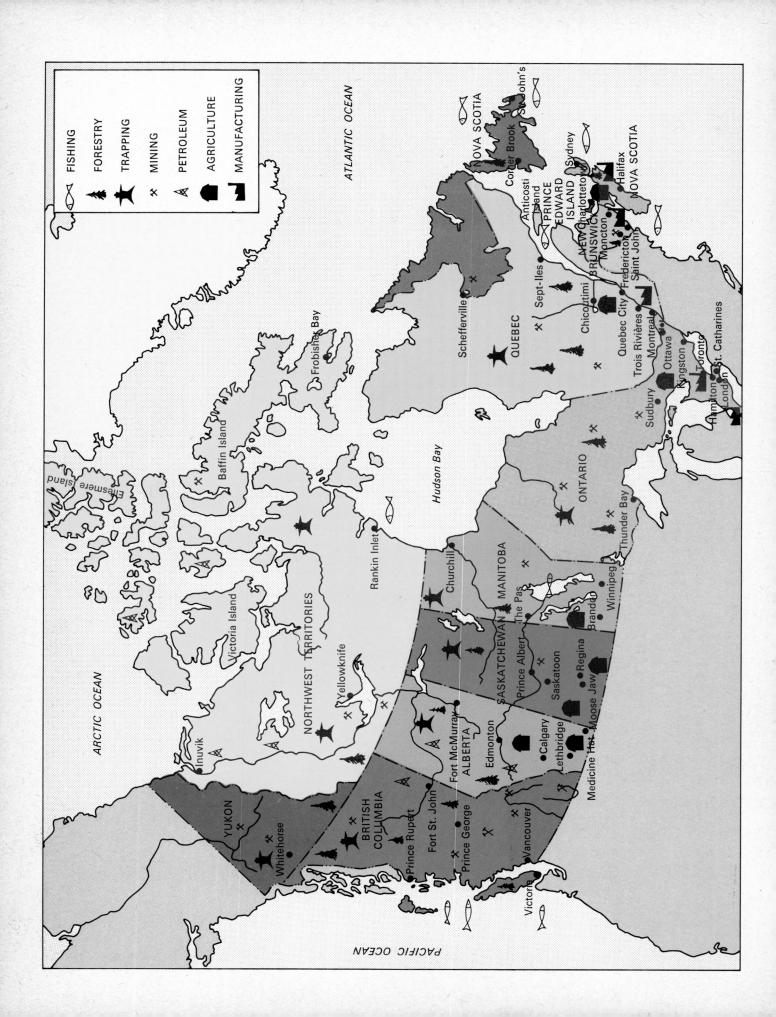

CONTENTS

CANADA

Canada is the world's second largest country, a giant of a land that fronts on three oceans and extends across seven time zones. As yet, most of it is a wilderness barely touched by man, for nine-tenths of its population live within 200 km of its southern border.

Early French visitors heard the term 'Kanata' from Indians of the St. Lawrence river. It means 'village,' but the French soon applied it to much of the land they knew as New France. Another part they named 'Acadia,' taking in what are now the Maritime provinces. The English settled 'Newfoundland,' and the Scottish 'Nova Scotia.'

'Labrador' is a corruption of the Portuguese words for 'land of slaves.' 'Quebec' is an Indian word for 'point of land,' first applied to the site of Quebec City and later to a whole province. Several more regions of Canada have Indian names. 'Saskatchewan' and 'the Yukon' (not to mention 'British Columbia') echo rivers; 'Ontario' and 'Manitoba' are associated with lakes.

one of her daughters. 'New Brunswick' is a reminder of the royal house of George III. The royal connection is brought up to date with the 'Queen Elizabeth Islands' of the Northwest Territories, named in 1953.

The royal place names recall Canada's special place in the world, a constitutional monarchy that is a leading member of the great family of nations known as the Commonwealth. Canada has drawn citizens from six continents, but the founding peoples came from only two — Indians and Inuit from Asia, French and British from Europe.

Besides the Commonwealth connection, Canada takes pride in its close relationship with its friend and neighbour, the United States. The long border between the two is undefended, and no other countries do as much business together. Canadians sometimes worry that they will be swamped by American culture, but to date they have held their own.

THE LANDFORMS

During the 1960s and 1970s, the world's geologists turned their science on its head. They accepted that the earth's crust consists of a number of independent plates floating like rafts on the hot mantle below. The plates respond to movements in the planet's interior, at times colliding with one another and at other times pulling apart.

The geologists have identified seven major plates and a number of smaller ones. Among the largest is the plate carrying the continent of North America, which consists of a thick layer of basalt rock topped by a heavy layer of granite.

The granite is most obvious in the ancient rocks of the Precambrian Shield that form the continent's core.

Precambrian rocks contain few fossil traces to show how old they are, but geologists say they could have been formed two billion years ago or earlier. Certainly they were in existence earlier than 600 million years ago. The geologists suggest that the rocks of the Shield were at the roots of ancient mountain systems worn away by erosion.

The Shield is exposed on the surface in a giant horseshoe cradling Hudson Bay, Canada's inland sea. It underlies the whole continent, but to the north, west, and south it is overlain by sedi-

ment, the product of erosion. Eastwards it extends to Labrador, where it reaches high elevations in the Torngat mountain range.

The sediments that overlie the Shield were deposited on the bottoms of ancient seas and lakes. Ceaseless erosion wore down the exposed rock of the Shield and older sediments, and rivers washed away the waste. Today, the strata rest one on another like the layers of a cake, some exposed on the surface, some hidden beneath it.

There are sediments in southern Ontario and southern Quebec, underlying the rich agricultural land found there. More sediments line the shores of Hudson Bay and continue under the sea. Others form Canada's prairies, the long tongue of the Mackenzie river valley reaching to the arctic, and the southern part of the arctic archipelago beyond.

The Shield and sediments were formed without interference from neighbouring crustal plates. Around Canada's perimeter, however, there has been continuous activity as plates come into contact or pull away. At least four foreign plates have had immense influence on Canadian landforms, two in the east, one west, and one north.

...e east, about 450 million years ...ate carrying North America ...tly with a plate carrying ...th Africa. The collision ...alachian mountain ...m Newfoundland ... worn down the ... were as high

...t and on
... are high
...cond colli-
...te. Farther
... its neigh-
...untains in
... up under
...eighbouring

...ral ways in
...uilt. In most

...a into eight
...sical features.

cases old rock is squeezed upwards by folding, or when a plate rides over its neighbour like a raft. Sometimes large expanses of old rock are lifted through expansion in the mantle. Only rarely are new mountains formed through volcanic activity.

All these methods are represented in the Cordillera of Western Canada, part of the chain of mountains that stretches all along the Americas' western sea-board. In Canada, the Cordillera consists of four or five parallel mountain ranges of which the Rocky mountains are a part.

The Rockies were formed by folding, and are among the newest mountains in Canada — a mere 50 million years old. That is why they remain starkly impressive compared with the rounded contours of mountains elsewhere. Ranges near the coast were thrown up as Pacific plates pushing eastwards dived beneath the continent.

The hard rocks of Canada's Precambrian Shield rise from the cold waters of Lake Superior. The Shield is the continent's geological core and consists of formations that are up to two billion years old or even more.

Glaciation

When more snow falls than melts, its own weight compacts its lower layers into ice. Several times in earth's history, so much ice has accumulated that the surface of the planet has been smothered by icefields. In places they have been two kilometres deep.

Under pressure from the snow above, ice in the fields became plastic, and was able to move. Reacting to gravity, the ice caps overflowed and glacial tongues (glaciers) spilled outwards towards the sea. Even though they moved very slowly, their huge weight gouged the rock beneath and scraped it clean of soil.

As the cold spell ended, the ice-fields melted, leaving massive debris behind them. Everywhere in Canada there are signs of their passing — drumlins and moraine hummocks in southern Ontario, potholes on the

prairies, snake-like eskers (the residue of meltwater rivers) over the barrens of the north.

Even today, remnants of the ice-fields linger at high altitudes and in the arctic. The Columbia icefield in the

Rockies, the Penny ice cap on Baffin Island, the Kluane icefield in the south-western Yukon — all continue to receive more snow than they lose through melting, and feed the glaciers that flow from them.

On northern Baffin Island, mountain peaks poke through the thick mantle of the Penny ice cap.

Three Oceans

There is more to Canada than meets the eye. North America's continental shelf extends beneath the sea, and under international law Canada controls its mineral resources. Besides, in 1977 Canada followed other countries' example in establishing offshore fisheries control zones of 200 nautical miles (about 370 km).

The fisheries control zones affect not only the Atlantic and Pacific oceans, but the northern sea as well. Canada's third ocean is often ignored, because for most of the year it is blocked by ice. However, new technology promises to open a sea lane across the top of the continent, perhaps in the near future.

Vacationers take advantage of Ingonish beach on Cape Breton Island, Nova Scotia.

In the Atlantic, the continental shelf carries a range of submerged hills known as the Grand Banks of Newfoundland, probably the world's finest fishing grounds. Other undersea formations include Georges Bank off Nova Scotia, rich in scallops but straddling Canada's border with the United States.

On the Pacific side, the continental shelf carries a whole range of offshore mountains of which Vancouver Island and the Queen Charlotte islands are parts. Again, the coast supports a rich fishery, and thousands of small islands and deep inlets prove irresistible to those who explore them in small boats.

LAKES AND RIVERS

For Canada, the most valuable legacy of the last ice age was the meltwater left behind as the glaciers retreated. Most of it has long since escaped to the oceans, but enormous quantities remain trapped in depressions on the surface.

According to one estimate, Canada possesses as much as one-quarter of all the fresh water on earth. Of course, much of it is bound up in ice caps and glaciers and long-term snowfields. Even so, enough remains to fill at least 563 lakes with a surface area of 100 km² or more, and tens of thousands of smaller ones.

Canada's largest lakes, Superior and Huron, are shared with the United States. So are Lakes Erie and Ontario. The largest lakes entirely within Canada are Great Bear Lake and Great Slave Lake in the Northwest Territories, followed by Lake Winnipeg in Manitoba and Lake Athabasca on the Alberta-Saskatchewan boundary.

As yet there has been no inventory of Canada's lakes. Thousands have never been visited, let alone named. Cartographers mapping a region of 13 711 km² south-west of Reindeer Lake in Saskatchewan identified about 7500 lakes, and an area of 15 773 km² south

Sunset in Shield country, northern Manitoba. The province holds tens of thousands of lakes, among them large stretches of water like Lakes Winnipeg and Winnipegosis.

and east of Lake Winnipeg holds about 3000.

Geographers sometimes define lakes as wide places in rivers, and most of Canada's fit the description. Typically, they receive water from several lesser rivers and empty into a larger one. The Churchill river of northern Saskatchewan and Manitoba is really a necklace of lakes linked by rapids.

The largest rivers draw their water from drainage basins covering thousands of square kilometres, separated from one another by heights of land. A few of the basins, notably the Saskatchewan system of the prairies and the Mackenzie system of the north, are entirely within Canada's borders. Most, however, are shared with the United States.

The most extensive of the basins is focussed on the Mackenzie river in the Northwest Territories, and covers one-fifth of Canada's land area. Besides the Mackenzie, it includes rivers like the Peace, Slave, and Athabasca, as well as thousands of lakes, including three of the largest in the country.

South of the Mackenzie system is the great basin that drains into Hudson Bay by way of the Nelson river. Its principal elements are the Saskatchewan river north and south, Lake Winnipeg and its sisters in Manitoba, the Winnipeg river that drains Lake of the Woods on the Ontario boundary, and the Red river flowing from the United States.

Both the Saskatchewan and the Mackenzie rivers have been important as transportation routes, but they are overshadowed by the St. Lawrence of Eastern Canada. The St. Lawrence draws nearly all its water from the Great Lakes, and delivers it to the huge sheltered gulf that serves as Canada's gateway to the Atlantic.

In New Brunswick, the St. John river basin drains into the Bay of Fundy. In British Columbia, the Fraser heads west to the Pacific while the Columbia departs into the United States. In the north,

the Yukon river crosses into Alaska, and travels more than 1000 km farther before it reaches the sea.

In places, man has interfered with rivers' flow by building dams to create artificial lakes. Some dams prevent flooding, as on the Columbia river in B.C.; some feed irrigation schemes, as in southern Alberta; the majority store water to generate electricity in a hydro station close by.

Lake Williston behind the Bennett dam on the Peace river; Lake Diefenbaker behind the Gardiner dam in Sas-

katchewan; the reservoirs of the Manicouagan development in Quebec — all these are examples of lakes created by man for special uses. Both on the St. Lawrence and St. John rivers, whole communities have been submerged.

Canada's water resources have been major influences on the national lifestyle. Farmers, fishermen, manufacturers, and power companies depend on them, and their roles in transport and domestic use are crucial. Besides, they have given their names to four provinces and the territories.

THE VEGETATION

Almost all of Canada was smothered by the glaciers of the final ice age, but some regions escaped. Among them were the tops of the Cypress Hills on what is now the Alberta-Saskatchewan boundary, and pockets in the western Yukon near the Alaska border.

It seems that trees, flowering plants, and other forms of vegetation survived in these regions, though obliterated elsewhere. As the glaciers melted and erosion produced soil, they helped to recolonize the surface of the earth. First lichens and then more complex plants advanced to the east and north.

In fact, the process is still going on. Lichens slowly work their way northwards across previously barren rock, helping to produce soil cover in which other plant life can take root. The plants colonize not only the land but the lakes too, slowly filling them with decayed matter until they become part of the dry land.

Lichens and miniature flowering plants carpet the arctic tundra, and in summer the plants provide a short-lived blaze of colour in the weeks of perpetual daylight. With them are stunted trees — arctic willow, birches, and alders that are really no more than shrubs. Living close to the ground, they escape the blast of winter blizzards.

Individual tree stands are found far in advance of the treeline, the artificial boundary drawn where average temperatures are high enough for trees to be sure of survival. The treeline snakes across northern Canada from the Mackenzie delta to Hudson Bay, and on towards the Atlantic.

South of the treeline, the forest cover becomes increasingly dense. Black spruce, white spruce, and tamaracks are typical of Canada's great boreal forest, part of a belt that stretches around the world. Nearly all the trees are conifers, except for the two deciduous species, birch and aspen.

The boreal forest crosses Canada from the Yukon to Newfoundland. South of it are a number of separate forest regions where tree cover depends on climate. In the eastern provinces, conifers mingle with deciduous species like red oak and sugar maple, and Ontario's Niagara peninsula used to support pure deciduous forest.

The 'prairies' are by definition the region once covered by grasses and forbes, a legacy of near-drought conditions in the area. Between the prairies and the boreal forest is a zone of parkland, where groves of aspen compete with the grasses for control of the central plains.

The Cordillera has vegetation patterns of its own. In the mountains, the forest gradually thins as it approaches the alpine treeline. The altitude of the treeline steadily drops towards the north, until in the arctic it is at sea level. On the Pacific coast, heavy precipitation helps species like the Douglas fir to grow strong and tall.

Moss and creepers cloak the trees of British Columbia's rain forests, as here on the Queen Charlotte islands.

A pattern of islands in Quebec's vast Mistassini provincial park. Each island is covered by trees of the boreal forest that crosses Canada and girdles the northern hemisphere.

The Climate

One way of analyzing climate is to measure the length of winter, defined as the period between the first major snowfall and the last. In more than 80 per cent of Canada, winter lasts longer than summer.

Only in the southern parts of the provinces are summers longer than winters. Farther north, plants still manage to thrive because daylight hours are longer. Above the treeline, however, there is no hot weather at all, because temperatures seldom rise above 18°C.

Fog in the Maritimes, rain in British Columbia, blizzards in Saskatchewan, sunshine in Alberta — each region of Canada has a reputation for certain weather patterns. Precipitation, temperature, wind, and humidity all contribute, and there are outside influences like the oceans, Hudson Bay, and the Great Lakes.

The large bodies of water tend to make winters warmer and summers cooler. Away from them, for instance on the prairies, temperatures plunge in winter and soar in summer. In Saskatchewan, winter days of −40°C are not uncommon, yet in summer the temperatures can climb to 35°C and even higher.

The central provinces receive the most snow in Canada — more than the arctic, which some geographers classify as a desert. The coastal fringes of east and west receive the most rain. The area that receives least rain apart from the arctic is the southern prairie region.

Precipitation aside, winter brings the freeze-up of rivers, lakes, and in the arctic, the sea. Conversely, the ice breaks up in spring, and the rivers again flow free. In southern Canada, fall cloaks the forest in yellows, reds, and many other shades, and most Eastern Canadians think of it as their favourite season.

With snowmobiles and sleds, Inuit families of the Northwest Territories cross the flat expanse of the arctic barren lands.

Provincial Emblems

The maple leaf is known the world over as Canada's symbol. Not so well known are the 12 floral emblems of the provinces and territories, which have been adopted as follows:

Newfoundland	Pitcher Plant
Prince Edward Island	Lady Slipper
Nova Scotia	Mayflower
New Brunswick	Purple Violet
Quebec	White Lily
Ontario	Trillium
Manitoba	Crocus
Saskatchewan	Prairie Lily
Alberta	Wild Rose
British Columbia	Dogwood
Yukon	Fireweed
Northwest Territories	Mountain Avens

A broad band of boreal forest divides the prairie and deciduous forest of the south from the treeless tundra of the north.

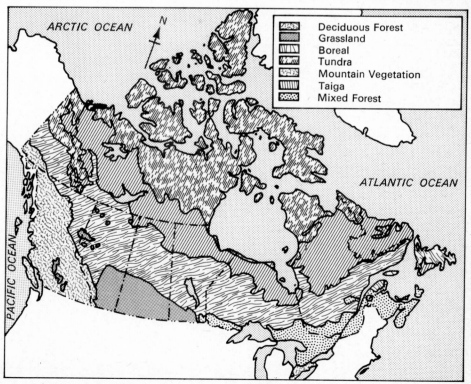

ARCTIC OCEAN

N

PACIFIC OCEAN

ATLANTIC OCEAN

	Deciduous Forest
	Grassland
	Boreal
	Tundra
	Mountain Vegetation
	Taiga
	Mixed Forest

The Sanctuaries

North America's oldest bird sanctuary is at Last Mountain Lake in Saskatchewan, set aside in 1887 to protect the nesting grounds of sandhill cranes. Point Pelee at Ontario's southern tip was set aside in 1918 to protect birds resting and nesting there after flying far from the south.

Canada's first reserve for animals was established in Alberta in 1906. Five Albertans volunteered to fence an area of the Beaver hills as a sanctuary for elk. The reserve was later enlarged to accommodate a herd of buffalo, and has since become Elk Island National Park.

Wood Buffalo National Park on the Alberta-Northwest Territories boundary; Quebec's Mistassini provincial park, set aside as a beaver sanctuary; Thelon game reserve in the N.W.T., a reserve for musk oxen of the interior — all over Canada, wildlife protection has been a major reason for setting aside public lands.

Outside reserves, wildlife is the responsibility of individual provinces and territories, but migratory birds are an exception. Since early in the century, the government of Canada and the United States have co-ordinated hunting regulations in the two countries. Besides, they co-operate to protect rare species from extinction.

ANIMAL KINGDOM

Arctic tundra, boreal forest, bald-headed prairie, Maritime marshland — Canada's climate produces a wide range of habitats, and each is enriched by its own assortment of wildlife. Some species are permanent residents, others come and go, but together they make the wilderness a naturalist's paradise.

There are roughly 185 species of mammals in Canada, among them 61 members of the rodent family. There are 35 species of snakes, and more than 500 species of birds. Some species, like the moose and beaver, are found from the Yukon to Nova Scotia. Some, like the Ipswich sparrow and pronghorn, are restricted to small areas. A few have been threatened with extinction.

Like many other Canadians, the Canada goose flies south for the winter. In spring it returns to nest in the arctic and on the shores of Hudson Bay.

Several of the most interesting species make their homes above the treeline. Shaggy musk oxen paw through the snow to find food, and form into a line or circle to deter potential aggressors. Barren ground caribou come together in migrant herds of tens of thousands to bear their young and mate for the next season.

Polar bears, the largest of Canada's mammals, hunt seals on the ice of the polar sea and in Hudson Bay. When the sea ice melts, most spend the summer

Southern Alberta and Saskatchewan used to hold large colonies of prairies dogs, but their numbers have declined seriously.

'Black' bears may well be brown, and are found in forest regions all across Canada. This one is in Kootenay National Park in British Columbia.

ashore, and the region south-east of Churchill in Manitoba is famous as a denning area. Canada holds roughly half of the world's polar bear population of about 20 000.

Tundra wolves hunt caribou and other prey; arctic foxes chase tiny lemmings the size of mice; tusked walrus and narwhals play in the polar sea; arctic terns reach their summer breeding grounds after flying all the way from the antarctic — the rich diversity of arctic wildlife helps man to survive where trees cannot.

The boreal forest stretches from the Yukon to Newfoundland, and has a population quite different from the north's. Woodland caribou move through the forest in small groups, and there are wood bison in northern Alberta. There are grizzly bears in the Cordillera and black bears are common across the country.

Moose, the largest members of the deer family, spend much of their time in water — not least to escape the flies of summer. A moose bull's spread of antlers makes it the most imposing animal in North America, though its ugly snout and splayed legs make it one of the least elegant.

Beavers, North America's largest rodents, create ponds deep enough not to freeze to the bottom during the coldest winter. There they store sticks and twigs as food supply. They also build lodges in which they raise their young, and engineer canals to help them move branches to their ponds.

Lynx, martens, fishers, otters, muskrats — the forest is full of valuable furbearers that have sustained generations of Indians and made white men rich. Mule deer and white-tailed deer are familiar too, and elk in the west, while smaller creatures like chipmunks and groundhogs are common across the country.

Bighorn sheep and mountain goats

are at home in the mountains of the Cordillera; cougars prowl British Columbia and parts of the Maritimes; herds of plains buffalo are protected in several national parks. On the Pacific coast, sea otters sport in the ocean, and there are colonies of sea lions off Vancouver Island.

Snow geese nest in the arctic archipelago, Canada geese on the shores of Hudson Bay. Birds of prey like peregrine falcons and gyrfalcons snatch smaller species as they fly. Bald and golden eagles soar over the mountains of British Columbia and Alberta, and black ravens and crows carry the spirits of ancient Indians.

Canada's fish population includes many members of the salmonidae family — five species of Pacific salmon, Atlantic salmon, arctic char, and steelhead trout among them. The salmon and char divide their lives between fresh water and the sea, though some have become landlocked and live permanently in fresh water.

Cod swim on Newfoundland's Grand Banks, giant bluefin tuna enter the Gulf of St. Lawrence, large shoals of herring swarm in the Bay of Fundy and off the B.C. coast. Whitefish, walleye, tullibee, and northern pike are among the fish commonly caught in the lakes of the interior.

A young moose browses in Alberta's Banff National Park. In summer, moose like to take to water to escape flies and other insects.

11

National Gallery of Canada

INDIANS AND INUIT

Parts of the western Yukon escaped the devastation of the final ice age. Archaeologists have found evidence that man lived in the region as early as 30 000 years ago, hunting mammoths and other creatures with tools made of bone.

The archaeologists surmise that the hunters had reached North America from Asia, crossing on a land bridge that once existed across the Bering strait. From the Yukon, the hunters probably spread southwards as corridors opened in the glaciers, and were followed by more peoples from Asia.

The pattern of early migration in North America remains a mystery, but over the centuries people adapted to their surroundings and developed distinctive lifestyles. In Canada, the Indians of the central plains lived by the buffalo, those of the forests by fish and furbearers, and those of the west coast by the salmon.

Ethnologists have identified eleven separate Indian language families in Canada, seven of them in British Columbia. There, tribes like the Haida,

An Indian encampment on the St. Lawrence opposite Quebec City, painted by Thomas Davies in 1788.

Kwakiutl, and Bella Coola developed a high level of civilization. Their elaborate totem poles and other carvings betrayed profound sensitivity to the spirit world around them.

Tribes of the interior had much less wealth, but the Bloods, Blackfoot, and Peigans built a military empire that was the scourge of the plains. Not until the eighteenth century was it challenged, when Cree entrepreneurs from the east entered the region on behalf of their French trading partners.

The Crees were one of the most complex tribes in Canada, a loose grouping of bands that stretched halfway across the country. They were frequently at odds with Indians who traded with the English, notably the Chipewyans of what is now northern Manitoba and the Northwest Territories.

Hurons lived in Ontario until decimated by Iroquois from the south; there were Micmacs in the Maritimes; there were Algonquian-speaking Indians in the interior of northern Quebec. Each

Public Archives Canada C-16336

Ontario's Indians used to play 'baggataway,' the ancestor of lacrosse. Some games involved up to 200 players on each side.

Public Archives Canada C-28858

Disguised as coyotes and toting bows and arrows, a pair of plains Indians stalk a herd of buffalo. A drawing by George Catlin.

people had proud traditions of its own, and its descendants are doing much to revive them.

Distinct from the Indians were the Inuit who lived north of the treeline, long known to white men as Eskimos. Like the Indians, the Inuit had crossed from Asia, but much more recently. They spread across the arctic from Alaska to Greenland, and learned to live from the bounty of the land of snow and the seas that surrounded it.

An early engraving of Inuit on the coast of Labrador, published in 1812. One baby rides in its mother's boot, a second in the hood of her parka.

Public Archives Canada C-25700

White Men

There were white men in North America long before Christopher Columbus landed in the West Indies. Basques from southern Europe may have settled in Nova Scotia as early as 500 B.C., and some historians believe that St. Brendan and a party of Irish monks reached Newfoundland in the sixth century A.D.

Before 1000 A.D., Norsemen from Scandinavia colonized Greenland and later founded outposts in North America. Remains of one of the early outposts have been uncovered at l'Anse aux Meadows on Newfoundland's northern peninsula. The Norsemen's adventures in what is now Canada are recorded in sagas that have survived to the present.

Perhaps in the fourteenth century, many of the Norse still in Greenland abandoned their settlements and re-established themselves on the Ungava peninsula of northern Quebec. Remains of their distinctive longhouses have survived, and there is evidence that they intermarried with local Inuit.

In the fifteenth century, English fishermen located land west of Iceland. In 1497 English merchants commissioned the Genoese navigator John Cabot to go and investigate. Like Columbus far to the south, Cabot discovered new territory and thought it was part of Asia. He claimed the 'Newe Founde Launde' for the English king.

Reports of Cabot's success led the Portuguese to send an expedition. It was led by Gaspar Corte-Real, who in 1500 and 1501 explored the coasts of Newfoundland and Labrador. Giovanni de Verrazano, an Italian in the service of the French, explored the coast of the mainland and named it *Nova Francia* or New France.

Besides discovering land, Cabot had noticed huge resources of fish on Newfoundland's Grand Banks. French and Basque fishermen converged on the region and landed on Newfoundland and the northern shore of the Gulf of St. Lawrence to prepare their catch. In addition, Basques came to the area to hunt for whales.

Europeans now believed that the 'islands' discovered by Cabot and others would be bypassed, and that the Asian mainland lay beyond. In 1534 the French sent another expedition, this time led by a Breton captain named Jacques Cartier.

French fishermen already familiar with local waters directed Cartier through the strait of Belle Isle that divides Newfoundland from the mainland. He went on to explore the Gulf of St. Lawrence, touching at Prince Edward Island and Anticosti and raising a cross in the Bay of Chaleur to claim the land for France.

Cartier returned to New France in the next year, and this time sailed up the St. Lawrence. There he visited two large Indian villages, one near the site of Quebec City and the other on Montreal island. In 1536 the French founded a small colony near Quebec City, but the settlers were withdrawn in the following year.

Old Acadia comes to life at Fortress Louisbourg on Cape Breton Island, partly reconstructed by Parks Canada and populated by interpretive guides who wear period costumes.

FRENCH AND ENGLISH

At the outset of the seventeenth century, Henry IV was king of France and James I was on the throne of England. Both monarchs saw the potential of the New World, and both gave enthusiastic support to subjects of theirs who wanted to found colonies.

The French king was first in the field. In 1603 he awarded a fur trading monopoly to Pierre du Gua, Sieur de Monts. The monopoly covered a wide region that the French termed Acadia, roughly speaking the Maritimes. De Monts organized an expedition of 125 men, among them the geographer Samuel de Champlain, and set sail in 1604.

The colonists entered the Bay of Fundy, and in the next year established Port Royal near the site of today's Annapolis Royal, Nova Scotia. The colony was later abandoned, but Champlain explored far afield. In 1608 he sailed up the St. Lawrence river and founded a 'habitation' on the site of Quebec City.

Champlain was to devote the rest of his life to New France. Meanwhile, the English (and Scottish) entered the field. In 1610 John Guy established the first 'plantation' on Newfoundland. In 1621 James I ignored French claims to the mainland and granted a large part of it to his friend Sir William Alexander.

A party of colonists was sent to 'Nova Scotia,' as Alexander named his domain. In 1629 three English freebooters, the Kirke brothers, captured New France. To their disgust, in 1632 the English made peace with France and returned the captured territory. At the same time, the Scottish colonists were recalled from Acadia/Nova Scotia.

The French were in control again, and their influence spread farther west. Trois Rivières was founded in 1634, Montreal in 1642. Jesuit missionaries entered the interior. Several of them were killed by marauding Iroquois, who were raiding Indians friendly to the French and disrupting the fur trade.

In 1663 New France was made a royal colony. The Carignan-Salières regiment arrived to protect the colonists against the Iroquois. Soon, the civil intendant Jean Talon was co-operating with Bishop François de Laval to introduce new settlers and develop agriculture in the colony.

In 1672 a new military governor was sent to New France — Louis de Buade, Comte de Frontenac. Under Frontenac, the French several times raided the English of New England, and their exploits won them the respect of the Indians. The fur trade prospered, the colony expanded, and New France seemed assured of a bright future.

The dream soon crumbled. The eighteenth century was to see continuing assaults by the New Englanders and the British too. In 1710 the New Englanders captured Acadia. In the whole maritime region, France was permitted to retain only its offshore possessions, notably what are now Cape Breton Island and Prince Edward Island.

On Cape Breton the French built Louisbourg, a major port and fortress to protect their fishing interests throughout the region. Louisbourg was supposed to be impregnable, but it fell into decay. In 1745 an invasion force from New England had little difficulty in capturing it.

To the New Englanders' dismay, in 1748 Britain returned Louisbourg to France. However, in the next decade relations between the two countries steadily worsened. There were conflicts in the interior as regular troops battled

Early in the eighteenth century the adventurers of New France reached the Red river in what is now Manitoba, seen here in Peter Rindisbacher's watercolour of 1822.

Public Archives Canada C-1938

The Fur Trade

Until about 1650, convoys of Huron entrepreneurs carried pelts to French settlements on the St. Lawrence. Then the trade route was disrupted by the Iroquois, who seized the Hurons' furs and carried them to Dutch and English traders in what is now New York.

To obtain furs, French traders had to venture into the interior. Among the most successful were Pierre Radisson and his cousin Médard Chouart, Sieur des Groseilliers. The cousins travelled as far west as Lake Superior and made contact with Hurons driven west by the Iroquois. The Indians agreed to collect furs from tribes that were even farther away.

Radisson and Groseilliers suggested to the French authorities that they could reach the interior more easily from Hudson Bay. The French were not interested, so the cousins turned to the English who soon afterwards formed a company. Chartered in 1670, it was given exclusive trading rights in 'Rupert's Land,' all the territory drained by rivers that emptied into the bay.

The 'Hudson's Bay Company' established trading posts on James Bay in the south and later on the west coast of Hudson Bay. In the 1680s the French began a long campaign to drive the

English away. First by land and later by sea, Pierre Le Moyne, Sieur d'Iberville, came close to success but never held all the English posts at one time.

Meanwhile, beaver fur was so fashionable in Europe that rival traders were spreading westwards to look for new supplies. The leading French adventurer was Robert Cavalier, Sieur de la Salle, who in 1682 descended the Mississippi river to the Gulf of Mexico. He claimed half North America for his sovereign and named it Louisiana.

On a broad river in Western Canada, brawny voyageurs shoot white water rapids on their route to the east. A painting by Frances Ann Hopkins.

In 1690 a servant of the Hudson's Bay Company, Henry Kelsey, was sent westwards to calm warring Indians. He reached what is now Saskatchewan. The French were exploring beyond the Great Lakes as well, and in the 1730s the La Vérendrye family from Trois Rivières reached what is now Manitoba and built a chain of forts.

on the Ohio frontier. In 1755, large numbers of Acadians were expelled from Nova Scotia.

In 1758 a British army and fleet besieged Louisbourg and forced it to surrender. The fortress was later dismantled. In the next year, the British beseiged Quebec. In spite of the brilliant leadership of Louis Joseph, Marquis de Montcalm, the French were defeated by the army led by Gen. James Wolfe.

In 1760 the British captured Montreal, and New France was finished. The Seven Years War ended in 1763. Under the Treaty of Paris France gave up all its possessions in Canada and Acadia except St. Pierre and Miquelon, two tiny islands off the south coast of Newfoundland.

Much of old Quebec City has been restored to look the way it did before the conquest of New France, as here in Place Royal.

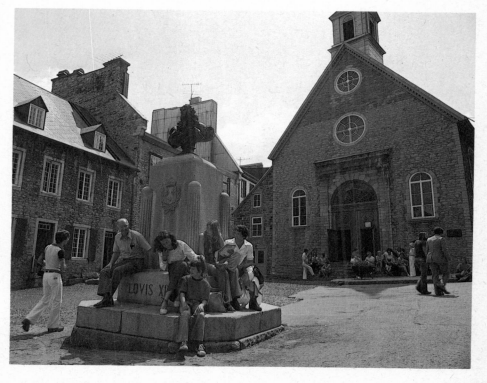

BRITISH NORTH AMERICA

No sooner were the British in control of New France or 'Canada' than aggressive English-speaking traders moved to Montreal. Within a few years, they and their representatives were travelling far to the west to meet the Indians and persuade them to begin trapping.

For a time it seemed that the French *habitants* of the St. Lawrence would be absorbed into a Protestant colony like the ones in New England. Then in 1774 the British parliament passed the Quebec Act. This gave the French important privileges, including the right to their religion and the right to their own civil law.

The Quebec Act expanded Canada's boundaries north-east to Labrador and west to the vast territory between the Mississippi and Ohio rivers. The English colonies saw this measure as an attempt to keep them to the Atlantic seaboard, and the Quebec Act was added to a long list of grievances.

Before long, the English colonies were in rebellion against Britain. They invited Nova Scotia and Canada to join them, but with no reaction. In 1775 the rebels invaded Canada, capturing Montreal and Trois Rivières and laying seige to Quebec City. The citadel held out, and in the next spring the invaders withdrew.

Nova Scotia and Prince Edward Island (a separate colony since 1769) suffered raids during the war, and when it was over Nova Scotia received many thousands of United Empire Loyalists fleeing the new republic. Many of the Loyalists settled north of the Bay of Fundy, and in 1784 they were permitted to create a new colony which they named New Brunswick.

The change to British rule made little difference to most of Quebec's *habitants*, who farmed strips of land extending back from rivers. A painting by Cornelius Krieghoff, 1856.

The Capital

One of Canada's most vexing questions during the 1850s was the choice of a national capital. Quebec City, Montreal, Kingston, and Toronto all had their supporters, and so did the young city of Ottawa. In 1857 the question was put to Queen Victoria for a final decision, and to the dismay of many she chose Ottawa.

Of course, there were sound reasons for the decision. Ottawa came close to straddling the boundary between Canada West and Canada East, so could be expected not to favour one over the other. Besides, Ottawa was far less vulnerable to attack from the United States than the four rival candidates in the south.

At this time Ottawa had a population of fewer than 8000, most of them depending on the local lumber industry. A railway connected the city with the shores of Lake Ontario, and there was a river link with Montreal. The Canadian government bought the site of Parliament Hill, approved elaborate designs for parliament buildings, and in 1859 called for tenders.

In 1860 the buildings' cornerstone was laid by the Prince of Wales, the future Edward VII. Ottawa filled with construction workers as the immense project got under way, with stone shipped by rail from Ohio and New York. Late in 1865 the Province of Canada's administration occupied the east and west wings of the new buildings.

Meanwhile, the legislature had been sitting in Quebec City. At first its members had been less than enthusiastic about moving to the 'wilderness,' as they assumed Ottawa to be. Gradually their mood changed, and in 1866 the legislature met in Ottawa and for the first time occupied its new quarters in parliament's centre block.

Other Loyalists arrived in what is now southern and eastern Ontario. In 1791 the British parliament passed the Constitutional Act by which Canada was divided into two provinces, Upper and Lower. The act emphasized the political division between the English in the west and the French in the east.

Meanwhile, traders from Montreal were challenging the trading monopoly of the Hudson's Bay Company. By the 1780s several groups of Montreal traders had come together as the North West Company, and their representatives were building forts in the Athabasca country of what is now Alberta.

In 1789 Alexander Mackenzie descended the great river now named after him, believing it would take him to the Pacific. In 1793 he ascended the Peace river and crossed the Cordillera. He reached the ocean at a point recently visited by the expedition of Capt. George Vancouver, who was exploring the Pacific coast for the Royal Navy.

Within a few years of Mackenzie's great expedition, Nor'Westers were building forts in British Columbia's interior. The Hudson's Bay Company entered the region too, and for years the rival enterprises fought tooth and nail to gain an advantage. Their fortunes were not improved by the Napoleonic wars, which cut off their European markets.

Much of the rivalry centred on the Red river colony in what is now Manitoba, founded by Lord Selkirk in 1811. Selkirk was a major shareholder of the Hudson's Bay Company, and his colony lay astride the supply routes used by the Nor'Westers. There were several serious clashes before 1821 when the two companies agreed to unite.

Farther east, Upper and Lower Canada had been embroiled in a war with the United States. Trying to capitalize on Britain's involvement in the Napoleonic war, Americans invaded Upper Canada in 1812 but were re-

pulsed at Queenston Heights on the Niagara peninsula. In the following year the Americans attacked and burned York, now Toronto.

The war ended in 1814, and its most lasting benefit was a feeling of nationality in the Canadas. The feeling was still strong in 1837, when there were separate rebellions in the two provinces to support demands for democratic rights. Upper Canada's rebellion was led by William Lyon Mackenzie, Lower Canada's by Louis Joseph Papineau.

The British quelled the insurrections with little difficulty, and soon appointed Lord Durham as governor-general of all five colonies of British North America. Durham recommended that the Canadas should be united and that Lower Canada's French should be

anglicized, for he saw no future for their culture.

In 1841 the British united the Canadas, but not in the way Durham suggested. Canada West and Canada East were given equal representation in a joint legislature, and their languages had equal rights. In 1849 the leading legislators were invited to form an administration, and the 'Province of Canada' had responsible government.

In 1858 gold was discovered on the Fraser river near the Pacific coast. Vancouver Island was already a colony, and the mainland was made the colony of British Columbia. Soon miners spread into the interior and discovered the rich deposits of the Cariboo, where the gold rush was to continue well into the 1860s.

NATIONAL CONVENTION

Canada West and Canada East had equal representation in their joint legislature. Administrations needed support in both, and frequently had two leaders to represent the opposing regional interests. The one that took office in 1858 was headed by John A. Macdonald of Canada West and George Etienne Cartier of Canada East.

Cartier had a large following, but Macdonald's was limited. That was why he welcomed the support of Alexander Tilloch Galt of Canada West, who had a revolutionary proposal. Galt wanted to bring about a union of all the colonies of British North America, and his idea was adopted as official government policy.

Canada West had good reason to seek such a union. The colonies no longer enjoyed preferential treatment in Britain, which had recently introduced free trade. Even so the Canadians' industries were growing and they needed a larger market at home. Besides, they wanted to improve transportation links with the other British colonies, and that meant joint railroad development.

For years there was no progress with the idea. Instead, the legislature concentrated on complaints from Canada West that it was under-represented. Its population was larger than Canada East's and a group from Canada West known as the Grits demanded a change in the constitution to permit the amalgamation of the two.

Prominent among the Grits was George Brown, editor of the Toronto *Globe*. For years he and Macdonald were bitter opponents, but in 1864 he proposed a coalition. He would join forces with Macdonald, Cartier, and Galt to reform the constitution by bringing about a union of all the colonies or of the Canadas alone.

By coincidence, in the same year the three Maritime colonies agreed to discuss a union of their own. No date had been set, but the administration of the Canadas asked to be allowed to send observers. The Maritime colonies agreed, and called a conference for Charlottetown in September.

The Canadas sent a delegation that included Macdonald, Cartier, Galt, and Brown. The Nova Scotian delegation was led by Charles Tupper, and New Brunswick's by Leonard Tilley. John Hamilton Gray led the men of the host colony. The conference met in Province House, seat of the Island legislature.

On the first day the Maritime delegates proposed their local union as arranged. Then curiosity got the better of them, and they agreed to let the Canadians take the floor. The Canadians wanted to outline their idea of a British North American federal union, and by the end of the week the Maritimers were eager to discuss it.

It was agreed that a 'national convention' should be held in Quebec City a month later. Meanwhile, the Canadians took the opportunity of touring the Maritimes to publicize their proposal.

Canada's most famous painting is Robert Harris's *Fathers of Confederation*, a reconstruction of the Quebec Conference of 1864 completed 20 years later. The original was burned in the fire that destroyed Ottawa's parliament buildings in 1916, but the painting survives in books and lithographs. The version shown here was commissioned by the Confederation Life Insurance Company in 1965 and was painted by Rex Woods. The new painting varies from the original in that it shows the Fathers as they appeared at the Quebec Conference, rather than as Harris pictured them 20 years later. Prominent among the Fathers are John A. Macdonald (standing before centre window); George Etienne Cartier (to his left); George Brown (seated, centre foreground); Charles Tupper (standing, right foreground); and Leonard Tilley (seated, left foreground).

They visited Halifax, Saint John, and Fredericton before rejoining their steamer and sailing up the St. Lawrence.

Besides the Canadians and Maritimers, two representatives of Newfoundland attended the convention in Quebec. The 33 'Fathers of Confederation' debated 72 resolutions introduced by the Canadians and passed them all. News of the resolutions was flashed to the interested colonies and was being discussed even before the delegates reached home.

Only in Canada West were the resolutions received warmly. In Canada East there were fears that they spelled the doom of French culture. Prince Edward Island and Newfoundland rejected them totally, fearing that union with the Canadas would overwhelm them. In Nova Scotia, Tupper faced

Border Problems

In 1861 civil war broke out in the United States. A few months later two agents of the Southern Confederacy were sailing to Europe on the British mail packet *Trent*. The packet was intercepted by an American ship and the agents were removed from it by force.

The *Trent* affair nearly provoked a war between Britain and the United States. The colonies of British North America prepared to resist invasion. The crisis was defused, but it reminded the colonies of the troublesome raids of 50 years earlier. Americans, it was plain, were not to be trusted.

In 1864, the tables were turned when southern sympathizers raided Vermont from Canada East. The Americans threatened to cancel their trade treaties with Canada, but before they did so the civil war was over. The colonies feared the victorious army of the Union states would be sent north to conquer yet more territory.

Fortunately the army dispersed. However, the United States did little to discourage the activities of the Fenian Brotherhood, an Irish nationalist or-

Public Archives Canada C-18737

Following the American Civil War, Canada was threatened by the Fenian Brotherhood, Irish nationalists based in New York who invaded Canada West in 1866. This is a fanciful lithograph of the Battle of Ridgeway.

ganization based in New York. By raiding British North America, the Fenians hoped to force Britain to grant Ireland's independence.

In spring 1866 a large force of Fenians entered south-western Canada West but were defeated by Canadian volunteers at Ridgeway. Later, Fenians prepared to attack Campobello Island in New Brunswick but were discouraged by British warships, while a party

that invaded Canada East from Vermont withdrew after a few days. Other raids were threatened, but by 1871 the Fenian movement was doomed to failure.

---

strong challenges from his political rival, Joseph Howe.

In New Brunswick, Tilley's Unionists had an election to fight and were defeated. For a time, that seemed to end the matter. Then the British government sided with Tilley and he was returned to power. A delegation from the Canadas, Nova Scotia, and New Brunswick went to Britain to negotiate the passing of an act of parliament.

The delegation reached London in 1866 and worked through the winter. At last an appropriate bill was prepared to their satisfaction. The British North America Act was passed by the British parliament, and received the royal assent on March 29. It came into effect by proclamation on July 1, 1867.

Suddenly, Canada was a Domin-

ion — a term suggested by Leonard Tilley, recalling the Biblical 'dominion that stretched from sea to sea.' Its former colonies became provinces — Nova

Scotia, New Brunswick, Quebec, and Ontario. Its capital, first occupied by a legislature only one year previously, was the City of Ottawa.

Canada as it appeared in 1873, six years after Confederation. The four original provinces were Ontario, Quebec, New Brunswick, and Nova Scotia. Manitoba became a province in 1870, British Columbia in 1871, and Prince Edward Island in 1873.

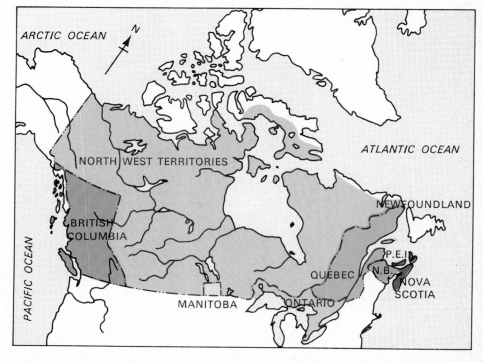

NEW TERRITORY

Even as they negotiated Confederation, Macdonald and his colleagues looked westwards to the vast expanse of Rupert's Land and British Columbia beyond. Macdonald aimed to create a dominion from sea to sea, and in the process to prevent the United States from laying claim to the empty prairies.

In 1868, the Hudson's Bay Company agreed to give up Rupert's Land in exchange for a cash settlement and the right to retain its posts and one-twentieth of all fertile land. In 1869 the Canadians prepared to take possession. Before they could do so, the mixed-blooded Métis of the Red river colony set up a provisional government under Louis Riel.

The Métis wanted an assurance that the Canadians would not destroy their way of life. The issue was complicated when the Métis executed an Ontarian surveyor, Thomas Scott, after attempts to overthrow their regime. Even so, the Macdonald government agreed to Métis requests, and in 1870 created the new province of Manitoba.

As first constituted, Manitoba was not much more than a postage stamp on the prairies, much smaller than it is today. All around it stretched the 'Northwest Territories,' westwards to the Rocky mountains, north to the arctic, and eastwards across what are now northern Ontario and northern Quebec.

Meanwhile, British Columbians were considering their future. The Cariboo gold rush was over, and in 1866 the mainland and Vancouver Island had been united as a single colony. Some of the colonists wanted to remain

An early lumber camp in British Columbia. Fallers attacked the giant Douglas firs with axes and crosscut saws, and teams of oxen dragged them to the nearest river.

independent, some wanted the colony to join the United States, and some wanted to join Canada.

The Confederation party gained strength in 1867 when the United States purchased Alaska from Russia. British Columbian delegates travelled to Ottawa to negotiate with the Canadians. The Dominion government agreed to take over the colony's debt, and to authorize construction of a transcontinental railroad to connect the west with the east.

British Columbia joined Confederation in 1871, making it Canada's sixth province. The seventh was to join two years later. Prince Edward Island, so long aloof from its colonial partners, was heavily in debt following construction of a trans-Island railroad. The Dominion agreed to take over the debt and provide transport to the mainland in all seasons.

The Island wanted to share the benefits of the Intercolonial Railway, being built by the Dominion government to link Quebec City and Halifax by way of New Brunswick. West of Quebec City there was already a network of railroads extending to southern Ontario, and the government was committed to continue it across the continent.

Early in 1873, soon after an election, Macdonald's government contracted a

The fur trade made Montreal rich, and it was the destination of many immigrants attracted from Europe. The scene behind Beausecours Market in 1866, as painted by William Raphael.

Public Archives Canada C-56481

Montreal syndicate to begin work on the railroad to the Pacific. The syndicate was led by a shipping magnate, Sir Hugh Allan. Unfortunately for Macdonald, it soon came to light that Allan had contributed campaign funds to members of his party.

Under the cloud of the 'Pacific Scandal,' Macdonald was forced to resign. The Conservatives were replaced by the Liberals led by Alexander Mackenzie (no relation to the explorer). The new administration set out to reduce government spending and promote exports, and at the same time raised tariff barriers to protect local industries.

Ignoring the previous government's commitment to British Columbia, the Liberals scaled down the transcontinental railroad project. British Columbians were told they would have to be content with a wagon road. There were loud protests, and Macdonald capitalized on it by unveiling a 'national policy' that won him the next election.

The national policy was really three policies in one. It promised country-wide development through higher tariffs (to encourage industry in the central provinces), an ambitious immigration policy (to populate the empty west and develop agriculture), and to complete the transcontinental railroad as a bond for all Canada.

In 1878 the Conservatives were re-turned to power by a landslide. Tariffs were raised, and government surveyors traversed the west to lay out townships for settlers. In 1881 another Montreal syndicate was awarded the charter to build the transcontinental railroad, and incorporated itself as the Canadian Pacific Railway.

The immense project was undertaken in three stages. One crew worked westwards from Winnipeg, grading the route and laying track across the prairies. A second crew worked eastwards from the Pacific coast. The western mountain ranges were a formidable barrier, but probably not so great as those faced by the crew working in the Shield country north of Lake Superior.

In spite of the obstacles, construction proceeded faster than scheduled. Much of the credit went to the American engineer in charge of western construction, William Van Horne. The eastern and western construction crews met at Craigellachie in British Columbia in 1885, and the last spike was driven home by a major shareholder, Donald Smith.

Fur traders bargain with Cree Indians at Fort Pitt in what is now Saskatchewan, early in the 1880s. The Cree in the centre is Big Bear, whose band was to play a leading role in the Northwest Rebellion of 1885.

National Photography Collection C-14154

LAST BEST WEST

Canada's purchase of Rupert's Land opened the way for settlement of the west. During the 1880s homesteaders from the poorer counties of Ontario took up land in Manitoba, and Mormon colonists from Utah crossed the international border to settle in southern Alberta.

At first, the pace of settlement was slow. Tens of thousands of migrants were arriving in Canada from Europe, but thousands more were leaving Ontario, Quebec, and the Maritimes to take jobs or seek free land in the United States. Many of those who remained preferred to seek work in Canada's cities rather than take their chances in the west.

John A. Macdonald was a national institution by the time he fought his last election campaign in 1891. He was victorious, but he died in the same year.

With the building of the new railroad, many more homesteaders crowded into the prairies. Most preferred to settle within reach of the main line, but gradually the new arrivals moved farther afield and branch lines followed them. Railroad camps like Regina, Moose Jaw, and Calgary quickly expanded and became cities.

In 1891 John A. Macdonald won his last election, and three months later he was dead. The nation mourned. Macdonald's successors squabbled among themselves and in 1896 were defeated by the Liberals. Canada's new prime minister was Wilfrid Laurier, a French-Canadian from Quebec.

Laurier's cabinet included Clifford Sifton from Manitoba, who masterminded a huge promotional campaign to attract new migrants. Canadian agents travelled all over northern Europe and Russia, distributing millions of pamphlets and posters prepared in a dozen

Public Archives Canada C-6536

THE OLD FLAG.
THE OLD POLICY.
THE OLD LEADER.

Law and Rebellion

In 1873 the Dominion government began recruiting a paramilitary force to maintain law and order across the prairies, the North West Mounted Police. After initial training in Manitoba, the force marched eastwards to clamp down on the activities of American whisky traders who were corrupting the Indians.

The NWMP, direct forerunners of today's Royal Canadian Mounted Police, established a chain of forts throughout the west. In many cases

they helped to persuade local Indian bands to sign treaties with the Dominion government. By these treaties the Indians gave up their land in return for cash and other considerations.

One of the police posts was Fort Carlton in what is now Saskatchewan, and it figured prominently in troubles that overtook the region in the 1880s. Like their cousins in Manitoba, local Métis wanted assurances that their lifestyle would not be destroyed. Louis Riel was persuaded to form a provisional government as he had in Manitoba, and a list of grievances was sent

to the Dominion government.

Ottawa was slow to respond, and during an affray near Fort Carlton the Métis killed a number of police and volunteers. The Métis were in rebellion, and so were two bands of Cree Indians dissatisfied with the treatment they were receiving under their treaties. The Dominion government immediately despatched troops to the west.

The troops were transported on the new Canadian Pacific Railway, complete but for four gaps north of Lake Superior. At Fort Qu'Appelle the troops divided into two columns, one to march on the Métis and the other to deal with the Crees. Meanwhile, a third force was being raised by the settlers of Alberta.

The Métis were heavily outnumbered, but through the military brilliance of Gabriel Dumont, they surprised the government troops at Fish Creek and stopped their advance. The Crees were successful too. Then the Métis were defeated at Batoche. Most of them surrendered, and so did the Crees. Louis Riel was convicted of treason and hanged in Regina.

The first Mounties relax after a day on the march in 1874, when they advanced westwards to police the plains.

languages. In addition, Canada advertized all over the United States.

Everywhere, Canada's prairies were being described as the 'last, best west' — 'last' in that there was no more free land in the United States. Britons, Germans, Americans, Scandinavians, Slavs, Russians, and Ukrainians poured on to the plains. Many arrived alone, many more arrived in family groups.

The townships laid out by surveyors in the 1870s were nearly ten kilometres square, and each was divided into 36 sections subdivided into quarter-sections. Homesteaders could take possession of a quarter-section by paying a fee of $10 and undertaking to remain on it six months of the year for three years.

As settlement spread, the Canadian Pacific Railway built branch lines. Even so, it could not satisfy demand, and it was plain Canada needed a second railroad farther north. The government received two proposals, and to its later embarrassment adopted both. Construction of the new lines began in the early years of the century.

Like the Canadian Pacific two decades earlier, the two new railroads

Throughout the nineteenth century, Indians, Métis, and whites continued to trap furbearers in the forests of the north.

Lees Dit! **(Dutch for "Read This!") The Canadian government and the Canadian Pacific Railway co-operated in a massive campaign to attract immigrants from Europe and the United States.**

raced across the plains. By 1905 the Canadian Northern had a line from Winnipeg to Edmonton, and prepared to continue to Prince Rupert on the coast of British Columbia. The Grand Trunk Pacific, linked to the Grand Trunk system of Eastern Canada, was to terminate at Vancouver.

Many homesteaders reached their land with few possessions, but neighbours helped one another and bred the tradition of western co-operation that survives to the present. Soon they were pressing for some say in their own affairs, and the government agreed to create two new provinces, Alberta and Saskatchewan, in 1905.

In the north, the two new provinces stretched to the 60th parallel, like British Columbia. Soon there were demands that eastern provinces should be enlarged too. The boundaries were redrawn, and in 1912 large regions of the old North West Territories were distributed among Manitoba, Ontario, and Quebec.

Meanwhile, in 1911 there had been an election. The Liberals had suffered serious losses in Ontario, and in Quebec their majority was seriously reduced by a new party, the *Nationalistes*. The key election issue in Quebec was a Liberal plan to build a Canadian navy, which might commit Canada to fight in Britain's wars.

A Canadian battalion 'goes over the top' during an offensive of 1916. Canadian troops saw action both in Flanders and in France.

FLANDERS FIELDS

Following the 1911 election, Laurier's Liberals were succeeded by the Conservatives. The new prime minister was a Nova Scotian, Robert Borden. When war broke out in Europe in 1914, Borden quickly assured the British that Canada would co-operate in whatever ways possible to win the war.

As hostilities began, the Canadian public was solidly behind the government. A War Measures Act giving the government extraordinary powers was passed unanimously. Volunteers flocked to recruiting stations and were sent to

Britain for training. By February 1915 there was a Canadian division in the trenches of Belgium's Flanders Fields.

Besides sending men to fight, Canada put industry to work to support the war effort. Factories turned out munitions, shipyards worked to capacity, and the mining and forest industries found ready markets for what they produced. Besides, Canada's farmers supplied food for Britain and the allies, and the whole economy prospered.

The first major battle in which Canadians were involved was the struggle for Ypres in 1915. French colonial troops on the Canadians' flank fell back, but the Canadians held firm and proved

their fighting qualities. Following the battle a second Canadian division arrived in France, and the two combined to form the Canadian Corps.

Lord Kitchener, in charge of the British war effort, wanted the Canadians to replace casualties in British regiments. The Canadian government preferred to keep the corps together as a unit, and undertook to keep it up to full strength. As a result, the Canadian divisions were used offensively more often than they might have been.

In 1916 the Canadians fought at the Somme, and lost more than 25 000 men killed, wounded, or missing. New arrivals brought the corps to a strength of four divisions. The corps scored its most notable victory at Vimy Ridge in April 1917, taking more ground and capturing more prisoners than in any previous 'British' offensive.

There were Newfoundlanders at war as well as Canadians, serving in the Newfoundland Regiment. They had served in the Gallipoli campaign of 1915 and at the Battle of the Somme. While the Canadians gained ground at Vimy Ridge, the fighting Newfoundlanders suffered terribly at Beaumont Hamel, where their strength was reduced from 735 to 68.

Newfoundlanders served in the Royal Navy too, and Canadians in the little Canadian navy that guarded the Atlantic coast from attacks by submarines. Several hundred Canadians joined the Royal Flying Corps, their chief purpose to fly as scouts, but whenever possible knocking their opponents out of the sky.

In June 1917 the Canadian Corps received a Canadian commander, Lt. Gen. Arthur Currie. He was soon called on to lead the Canadians in the mud of Passchendaele. The Canadians secured the ridge that was their objective, but in the process lost 15 000 casualties.

The Germans organized one last

One night in February 1916, fire swept the centre block of Ottawa's parliament buildings and destroyed all but the library. This was the scene on the following morning.

A caravan of packhorses and their attendants stand amid the ruins of a town in Flanders as they prepare to carry ammunition to Canadian artillery.

offensive in the spring of 1918. The Canadians were closely involved in the allied counter-offensive that followed it, pursuing the retreating Germans back to their homeland. At last there was an armistice. In 1919, Canada's prime minister joined other allied leaders in signing the Treaty of Versailles.

At home, the Canadian government had been hard pressed to keep the Canadian Corps up to strength. By the end of 1916 it was forced to consider conscription, and introduced it in 1917. English Canadians, loyal to the king and to Britain, supported it enthusiastically. French-Canadians bitterly opposed it.

Meanwhile, one of Canada's most upsetting losses of the war years had nothing to do with the fighting. One night in February 1916 a fire started in parliament's centre block, and by morning it was devastated. Only the library survived, and the government had to order complete reconstruction that would not be completed until 1920.

Counting the cost of the war, nearly 700 000 Canadians and Newfoundlanders had enlisted in the armed forces, and some 62 000 lost their lives. At the time, Canada and Newfoundland had a combined population of only eight million. It was recognized that their contributions were out of all proportion to their size.

Military Traditions

In 1871 the British withdrew all their forces from Canada, apart from small garrisons at their naval dockyards in Halifax and Esquimalt on Vancouver Island. Canada prepared to defend its own borders and formed the nucleus of a permanent defence force.

The permanent force was too small to stand on its own, so in 1872 Canada passed the Militia Act. Many thousands of volunteers were enrolled and trained in annual camps. In 1883 the government authorized an increase in the permanent force, and sent both troops and militia to put down the Northwest Rebellion in 1885.

A year earlier, a force of about 400 Canadian voyageurs had taken part in the attempt to relieve Gen. Charles Gordon at Khartoum on the Nile. Their job had been to guide the expedition's boats past rapids. In 1898 a contingent of militia — the Yukon Field Force — was sent to the Klondike to help control the gold rush.

Several Canadian contingents went to war in South Africa at the turn of the century. The Canadians fought on the side of the British in their struggle against the Boer commandos of the Transvaal and Orange Free State.

When the Boer War broke out in South Africa in 1899, many English Canadians wanted Canada to send a force to fight for the British Empire. French-Canadians opposed the idea, believing it was none of Canada's business. Laurier's government compromised by agreeing to equip and transport a force of not more than 1000 volunteers.

In time, more than 7000 Canadians fought in the Boer War, and many saw action in the decisive battles. Meanwhile, there was tension in Europe. Britain and Germany were racing to increase their naval power, and Britain was concentrating its forces at home. The naval dockyards in Canada were presented to the Dominion government.

In 1910 Canada began assembling a navy of its own. Two cruisers were bought from the British to serve as training vessels. Canada intended to build a number of new ships or to contribute funds to the Royal Navy, but nothing further was done until after the start of World War I.

National Photography Collection C-29310

THE DEPRESSION

Following World War I, Canada suffered a severe depression. Industrial workers sympathetic to the recent revolution in Russia formed 'One Big Union' (OBU), pledged to create a socialist state. Farmers entered politics too, and formed their own parties to press for reduced freight rates and combat high interest charges.

The OBU had its first test in Winnipeg, where in 1919 it supported a general strike. Workers were out for six weeks, but the strike ended in violent confrontation and they went back to work. The leaders were arrested, the threat of radical action faded, and socialists turned to less inflammatory methods to promote their causes.

The farmers had more success. In 1919 the United Farmers of Ontario won the provincial election in that province. In 1921 they were followed by their counterparts in Alberta, and in 1922 by the farmers of Manitoba. In 1920 the various farmers' parties had pooled their resources to fight federal elections as the National Progressive Party.

The Progressives showed great strength in the federal election of 1921, but their support fell away as Canada's economic position improved. The 1920s were dominated by the Liberals led by Mackenzie King, a grandson of the William Lyon Mackenzie who led the Upper Canadian insurrection of 1837.

King was shrewd and able, and he presided over swift advances in Canada's industrial strength. Highways and railroads were upgraded, hydroelectric facilities were installed, and large sums were spent on new mills and factories. Most regions depended heavily on primary industries, but manufacturing was strong in Ontario and Quebec.

Then came the economic crash of 1929, when all North America was plunged into depression. Industries failed, and the unemployed demanded relief. King insisted there was little he could do for them, and in 1930 his

The difficulties of the 1930s spawned several new political movements. One was the Co-operative Commonwealth Federation of the west. Here the party holds an open-air meeting in a park in Regina.

Liberals were defeated by the Conservatives. The new prime minister was a lawyer from Calgary, R. B. Bennett.

The Conservatives hoped to improve Canada's prospects by developing new trade ties with Britain. However, whole industries were in trouble. The demand for newsprint, Canada's leading export, was a fraction of what it had been. Fish sales were down, and so was the value of minerals and of wheat from the prairie farmers.

On the prairies, the depression was complicated by a drought that was to last until 1937. In some regions no rain fell for years on end, and the precious topsoil was blown away in clouds of black dust. Whole families left the land to move elsewhere, perhaps to British Columbia or the Peace river country of northern Alberta.

In many cases, young men left home so that there would be one less mouth to feed. They joined a growing army of unemployed who migrated from city to city, hopping freight trains and sleeping rough. Many communities established relief kitchens to provide soup for the young men and perhaps gave them a place to sleep.

The Conservative government's economic policies fell far short of improving matters. The cities of Eastern

During the depression years, many of the unemployed were accommodated in relief camps like this one at the air station in Ottawa.

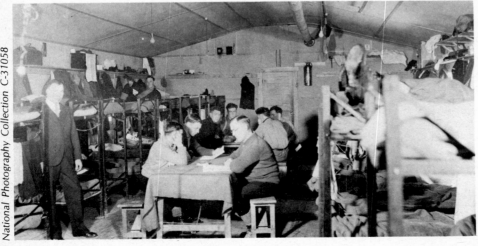

National Photography Collection C-31058

Canada suffered less than most, because their factories were producing for a captive domestic market and supplied many jobs. The primary industries of the countryside depended on exports, but there were no markets for what they produced.

To cope with the unemployed, the Dominion and provincial governments organized a number of make-work projects across the country. In return for their keep, the unemployed laboured on projects like highway construction. In 1935 a number of those on relief work in Vancouver went on strike and decided to march on Ottawa.

A train was commandeered to carry the protesters, and their numbers swelled as they crossed the country. The government stopped them at Regina, though a few delegates were allowed to take their grievances to the capital. Meanwhile, the other 'trekkers' tangled with the Royal Canadian Mounted Police in the 'Regina riot.'

General dissatisfaction gave impetus to three political protest movements. One was a socialist organization that eventually won election in Saskatchewan, the Co-operative Commonwealth Federation (CCF). The second was Social Credit, an attempt to stimulate consumer spending that took the party to power in Alberta in 1935.

The third protest movement was the Union Nationale of Quebec, a coalition of several parties led by Maurice Duplessis. As founded, the party was committed to social reform. On that promise it was swept into office in the Quebec provincial election of 1936, but it soon linked hands with the all-powerful church and Quebec's business community.

There was a general election in 1935, and both the CCF and Social Credit won seats. More important, Bennett's Conservatives were defeated by Mackenzie King's Liberals. Even with a new government the economy remained stagnant. King commissioned an important study of federal-provincial relations that recommended a fairer distribution of wealth.

National Photography Collection C-29399

Statute of Westminster

Every few years, leaders of self-governing nations within the British Empire came together to discuss imperial policies. Besides Britain and Canada, the nations were South Africa, Australia, New Zealand, the Irish Free State, and Newfoundland.

At the conference called in 1926, Mackenzie King of Canada asked for clearer definitions of imperial relationships. A commission was appointed to study the question, and its report spoke of a commonwealth of nations 'in no way subordinate one to another in any aspect of their domestic or external affairs.'

It was agreed, however, that the nations would retain their common allegiance to the Crown. Details were hammered out at the imperial conference of 1930, and in 1931 the British parliament passed the Statute of Westminster, giving the proposals the force of law. The legislation freed the dominions from the possibility of British control, though the British Privy Council remained the empire's highest court of appeal.

Among rights conferred by the statute, dominions were allowed to pass whatever legislation they liked, whether or not it conflicted with English law. Besides, their constitutions were confirmed, and they were given absolute control over the conduct of their affairs outside their borders as well as inside.

To Victory! The fierce Canadian beaver aligns itself with the British lion. Propaganda posters like this one helped to build Canadian morale and inspire patriotism.

WAR AND PEACE

In September 1939 Britain and France declared war on Germany. A week later Canada followed suit. A division of Canadian troops was sent to Britain, and the government set to work to strengthen the armed forces and rally the country to support them.

At the war's outset, Canada had a tiny air force, an even smaller navy, and a modest army of a few thousand personnel. Soon, recruiting stations were inundated by young men still out of work or looking for the chance of adventure. At the same time, factories were converted to produce munitions and other supplies.

The first months of the war were an anti-climax, for little happened. Then Germany began its *blitzkrieg* of Western Europe. France fell, and Britain itself came under heavy attack. Until the United States entered the war, Canada was to be Britain's most significant ally both in a military sense and as a supplier.

As the war progressed, the navy expanded from its original 15 vessels to nearly 500, among them aircraft carriers, cruisers, destroyers, frigates, and corvettes. Personnel increased from fewer than 2000 to about 100 000, who figured prominently in protecting the Atlantic sea lanes from the menace of German submarines.

Canada's air force began the war with 4500 men, and one squadron reached Europe in time to fight in the Battle of Britain in 1940. Subsequently nearly 50 Canadian squadrons took part in operations over Europe. Fifteen were bomber squadrons, the remainder were fighters, and all were placed under the control of the Royal Air Force.

By the war's end nearly 250 000 men and women had served in the Royal Canadian Air Force. Many of the pilots learned to fly at schools of the Commonwealth Air Training Plan in Ontario and on the prairies. With them were thousands of trainee pilots from Commonwealth countries, the United States, and countries occupied by the enemy.

Newfoundland

The depression of the 1930s affected Newfoundland even more profoundly than it did the prairie provinces. In 1934 Newfoundland's self-government was suspended, and the premier and his cabinet were replaced by a commission appointed by the British.

The commission was responsible not only for the island of Newfoundland, but for mainland Labrador too. Newfoundland's control of Labrador had been confirmed by a decision of Britain's Privy Council in 1927, running contrary to the claims of Canada. Labrador's boundary was said to run along the height of land that separated it from Quebec.

Newfoundland survived the 1930s, and became prosperous in World War II. Fishermen made money, and so did those who worked on military bases established by Canada and the United States. The commission banked tens of millions of dollars in case the war was followed by another recession like the one of the 1930s.

After the war a 'national convention' was called to decide what course Newfoundland should take. Some delegates wanted the status quo to continue, some wanted to revert to self-government. A small group led by Joey Smallwood suggested a radical alternative, Confederation with Canada, which at first attracted little enthusiasm.

The delegates could not agree, so in 1948 they put the question to the people in a referendum. Voting was so close that a second referendum was organized. The result favoured Confederation over Dominion status by 52 per cent to 48 per cent. In March 1949, Newfoundland became Canada's tenth province with Smallwood as its premier.

On Newfoundland's admission to Confederation in 1949, Canada's prime minister Louis St. Laurent begins the work of carving the new province's arms on the great arch of parliament.

Bodies, tanks, and an abandoned landing craft are mute testimony to the disaster of the Dieppe raid of 1942, in which Canadians suffered devastating losses.

National Photography Collection C-14160

Both the navy and the air force played positive roles in the war from the beginning, but for the army there were frustrations. Canadian troops were in Hong Kong in 1941 when it fell to the Japanese, and in 1942 Canadians suffered terrible losses during the abortive raid on Dieppe on the French coast.

In 1943, a Canadian infantry division and a tank brigade took part in the successful invasion of Sicily, and the Canadian Corps was given some of the most difficult assignments of the Italian campaign. In 1944, the First Canadian Army took part in the D-Day landings in Normandy, and pressed towards a rendezvous with the corps.

By the war's end, 750 000 men and women had served in the army. The effort of keeping it up to strength had come close to toppling Mackenzie King's Liberals, who had been forced to break a promise not to introduce conscription for service outside Canada. In Quebec, there were widespread protests.

Meanwhile, Canadian industry had risen to the challenge of keeping the forces supplied. Both primary and secondary industries contributed even more than they had in World War I. New technology was introduced, and Canada ended the war with a flourishing economy that gave it a head start in the peace.

One lasting effect of the war was to strengthen Canada's relationship with the United States. Even before it started, the two countries had promised to help defend each other. While it was in progress, their mutual trade increased dramatically, and they agreed to cooperate in their production for the war effort.

Canada allowed the United States to operate air bases on Canadian territory and even to build a highway to Alaska

Throughout World War II, Canada helped Britain to liaise with the United States. Twice the three countries' leaders conferred in Quebec City, as here in 1943. Seated from left are Mackenzie King of Canada, Franklin Roosevelt of the United States, and Winston Churchill of Britain.

by way of British Columbia and the Yukon. Besides, the Americans built the Canol pipeline from the Mackenzie river delta to the Yukon to ensure that Alaska did not run short of fuel.

Like the other countries that had won the war, Canada was a founding member of the United Nations Organisation founded in 1945. In 1949 it joined NATO, the North Atlantic Treaty Organisation. In the next year, Canada

agreed to send troops to South Korea, helping to stave off communist invasion from the north.

Canadians spent three years fighting in Korea, and about 25 000 of them saw service there before a truce was called. Once more, Quebeckers served notice that they would not tolerate conscription. In English Canada, the war aroused strong feelings against Canadian communists and their ideals.

National Photography Collection C-1700

29

CENTENNIAL

Mackenzie King retired in 1948 and died two years later. His successor was Louis St. Laurent, formerly his lieutenant in Quebec. St. Laurent's government placed less emphasis on Canada's long-standing links with Britain, and cultivated new economic relationships with the United States.

By the mid-1950s, the Liberals had been in power for 20 years without interruption. They were efficient, but were criticized for arrogance towards parliament. A new Conservative leader, John Diefenbaker from Saskatchewan, championed the rights of the electorate and in 1957 scored an upset election victory.

Nearly lost in the crowd, Pierre Elliott Trudeau is chosen to succeed Lester Pearson as leader of the Liberal party and prime minister of Canada. It happened in the year following Expo 67.

Quiet Revolution

All Canada's regions have a life and history of their own, but Quebec's are the most distinct. In 1959 Quebec embarked on a 'quiet revolution' following the death of Maurice Duplessis, who had dominated provincial politics since the 1930s.

Duplessis had allied himself with the church and Quebec's business interests, but had been an implacable foe of federal governments. His successors in the Union Nationale cautiously introduced a program of social reform, and the movement briskly accelerated when the Quebec Liberals won power in 1960.

The Liberals urged Quebeckers to become '*maîtres chez nous*,' 'masters in our own house.' One way was to lessen the influence of the church, achieved when the provincial government took control of education and social services. Another was to renegotiate Quebec's financial relationship with Ottawa, increasing its independence.

The 'quiet revolution' was accompanied by a dramatic upsurge in creative expression. Musicians, writers, painters, and filmmakers celebrated Quebeckers' new freedom and never had French-Canadians been so conscious of their potential. Their mood was infectious, and was one of the greatest assets of Expo 67.

Before long, Quebec exuberance led to demands that the province should separate from Canada. The mood was given public expression when Gen. Charles de Gaulle, president of France, visited Montreal in 1967. Standing on a balcony, De Gaulle proclaimed: '*Vive le Québec! Vive le Québec libre!*'

Quebec's revolution was no longer quiet. In 1970 young terrorists of the *Front de Libération du Québec* (FLQ) kidnapped a provincial cabinet minister and later assassinated him. The crisis was resolved, but not before English Canada realized Quebec's demands had to be taken seriously.

Montreal's city hall, where in 1967 Gen. Charles de Gaulle called out: '*Vive le Québec libre!*'

Diefenbaker formed a minority government, and a few months later strengthened his position with a massive election victory that swept the country. His administration introduced a Canadian Bill of Rights to protect the individual, and laid plans to open Canada's northland by building 'roads to resources.'

Unfortunately for Diefenbaker, there was dissension in his cabinet. The regional interests of the prairies conflicted with those of Eastern Canada, and Diefenbaker himself could make little of Quebec. In the election of 1962, public support of the Conservatives was dramatically reduced, and in 1963 they were swept from office.

The Liberals returned to power, but with a minority government. Their new leader was Lester Pearson from Ontario. Formerly a diplomat, Pearson had won the Nobel Peace Prize of 1957 for his efforts to resolve the Suez crisis of the previous year. Now he set out to revive the traditions of King and St. Laurent.

In spite of another election in 1965, Pearson never did win a parliamentary majority. He had to tread cautiously in the face of opposition from the Conservatives and two smaller parties. One was the New Democratic Party, formed from the shell of the CCF. The other was Social Credit, now popular in Quebec.

Pearson was in power in 1967, the year of Canada's centennial. The whole nation celebrated, and everywhere communities organized special projects. Arenas were built, gardens laid out, swimming pools excavated. Winnipeg hosted the Pan American Games; the national capital lit a 'centennial flame' on Parliament Hill.

The showpiece of centennial celebrations was Montreal's Expo 67, a 'first-category' exhibition designed as 'a living testimony to the contemporary epoch.' The idea had been proposed following the Brussels world's fair in 1958, and years of work went into construction of a man-made island in the St. Lawrence.

Some of Expo's pavilions were thematic, illustrating aspects of 'Man and His World.' Man the Explorer, Man the Creator, Man the Producer, and Man in the Community were all represented. Other pavilions were erected and organized by individual nations and groups of nations, states, provinces, and private sponsors.

For many visitors, Expo's greatest attraction was its feast of architecture. Never had so many innovations been assembled on a single site. West Germany's pavilion was a tent, translucent plastic slung from oblique poles. Mexico built a starshell of wood and aluminum, and Israel's pavilion was cubist.

The United States contributed a giant sphere that represented the globe; India's pavilion copied a huge sun-dial in New Delhi; Japan's looked like a gigantic log cabin. Perhaps the most remarkable building of all was Habitat, a new concept of apartment living that combined urban convenience with rural privacy.

More than 50 million visitors trooped through Expo in the summer of '67. They learned from the pavilions, they had fun in La Ronde, the midway. More than anything, they became aware of an extraordinary vitality in Quebec

Among scores of architectural marvels at Montreal's Expo 67 was an enormous transparent dome that housed exhibits from the United States.

and in Canada, something that promised wonders for the future.

Canadians themselves were taken by surprise. All the world's achievements were represented at Expo, and yet Canada's arts and sciences were plainly of the first rank. Canadians had always seen themselves as staid and perhaps boring. Now they took another look and decided their nation was exciting.

Lester Pearson resigned in 1968, but Expo euphoria was still much in evidence. Many observers believe it lay behind the choice of Pierre Elliott Trudeau as Pearson's successor. Trudeau's flamboyance ran against the Canadian tradition, and the national Trudeaumania that accompanied his selection showed Canadians expected him to keep alive the spirit of '67.

THE ECONOMY

Long before white men arrived, Indians and Inuit lived by fishing, hunting, and trapping. Hurons of what is now Ontario grew crops, and in several regions Indians mined native copper to make cutting tools. In the Rockies, Indians cut 'lodgepole' pines to make poles for their lodges.

Examples like these show where Canada's great primary industries had their start. Trapping, fishing, agriculture, forestry, and mining are all rooted deep in the past. So is Canada's reliance on trade, for Indians often carried surplus products for huge distances to regions where they were valued.

Existing trade patterns were a great help to the early settlers of New France. Before Iroquois began raiding, the French had no need to stir from the St. Lawrence, and relied on Huron entrepreneurs to do most of the work. Even today, the trapping industry depends heavily on Indians, Inuit, and Métis.

Europeans entered the fishing industry even earlier than they launched their fur trade. Basque and French fishing vessels were active on the Grand Banks of Newfoundland before Jacques Cartier explored the Gulf of St. Lawrence. On the Pacific coast, salmon fishing has been a staple of the economy for untold centuries.

The first European farmer in Canada was Louis Hébert, a Parisian who settled at Tadoussac on the St. Lawrence in

The lobster season earns handsome incomes for inshore fishermen in the Maritimes, like these off Shippegan in New Brunswick.

1617. Later, French *habitants* cleared rows of strip-farms along New France's rivers, and there were similar arrangements in Acadia, where settlers dyked marshes to create new land.

In New Brunswick and Ontario, the pioneer settlers had to cut into the forest to create their farms. On the prairies, they had to plough up thick sod. Improving technology helped their descendants to take on more work with less help, and today only a small fraction of Canada's population is employed in agriculture.

The trees cut down by settlers to clear land were burned to produce potash, Canada's earliest forest export. Later, prime trees of Quebec and the Maritimes were felled to serve as ship's masts and spars, and squared timbers and 'deals' — boards cut to standard dimensions — were exported to both Europe and the United States.

The first European mining ventures in Canada were not promising. In the 1530s Jacques Cartier found what he thought were gold and diamonds on the St. Lawrence, but was soon proved wrong. In the 1570s, the English explorer Martin Frobisher three times

Canada's farmers are assisted by major research programs at universities and agricultural research stations. At the University of Manitoba in Winnipeg, a researcher tests new varieties of grain.

Central Banking

Canada's economy revolves around eleven chartered banks that together supply most of the cash available for circulation. Ninety per cent of their assets are controlled by the 'big five' — the Canadian Imperial Bank of Commerce, the Royal Bank of Canada, the Toronto-Dominion Bank, the Bank of Montreal, and the Bank of Nova Scotia.

Behind the chartered banks stands the Bank of Canada, the Crown corporation directly responsible for the nation's monetary policy. The central bank was founded in 1934 to regulate credit and currency, control and protect the external value of the Canadian dollar, and offset fluctuations in the economy.

The central bank has no direct business with the public at large. Instead, it deals with the chartered banks and with the government. By law, the chartered banks are required to deposit set portions of their reserves with the Bank of Canada, and the bank serves as banker and fiscal agent for the whole of the federal administration.

The central bank regulates credit in the country as a whole by varying the money supply available to the banking system. By increasing the cash reserves in the system, it can attempt to force down interest rates, thus stimulating borrowing and spending by the public. By decreasing the reserves, the opposite should happen.

Besides its other responsibilities, the Bank of Canada acts as agent and adviser in managing Canada's reserves of foreign exchange. These reserves can be traded on international markets, and by doing so the central bank can influence the value placed on the Canadian dollar by nations around the world.

Energy shortages have prompted mining companies to step up their search for uranium. Here, a geologist uses a geiger counter to check rocks in the interior of British Columbia.

carried cargoes of 'fool's gold' home from Baffin Island.

Fortunately, later efforts were more rewarding. Coal was mined in what is now New Brunswick in the 1640s, copper on the Gaspé peninsula in the 1670s, bog iron near Trois Rivières from the 1730s. The Cariboo (1860s) and Klondike (1898) gold rushes were symptomatic of scores of less publicized mining ventures that have made Canada rich.

Minerals, trees, soil, fish, and furbearers are among Canada's principal assets, and with them fresh water in its many applications. One of the most important is hydro power, the harnessing of scores of rivers and lakes to provide cheap electricity for many purposes, not least industrial.

Cheap hydro power has enabled Canada to become one of the world's leading smelters of aluminum, the only major metal not mined in Canada. It is also a great boon to the pulp and paper mills that provide Canada's most valuable manufactured exports, and other great industries like nickel

and copper smelters.

The earliest of Canada's large-scale manufacturing industries relied not on cheap power but on craftsmanship. Through most of the nineteenth century, Quebec and the Maritimes held hundreds of small or medium-sized shipyards that built cargo vessels for European owners or for local merchants.

Wooden ships gave way to iron and steel. Even so, the shipbuilding tradition lingers in the eastern provinces and in British Columbia too. Shipbuilding is only one of hundreds of manufacturing industries that serve Canada's domestic markets and produce a substantial surplus for the world market.

Behind the primary and secondary industries stands a huge reserve of service industries, which employ the great majority of the labour force. Many of the most productive are concerned with the tourism industry — hotels, restaurants, and other establishments that attract foreign visitors to Canada, and with them their currency.

Increasing leisure time has made tourism an important industry all across Canada. On Prince Edward Island, one of the leading attractions is the Anne of Green Gables homestead near Cavendish.

33

Fish and Fur

Codfish attracted Europeans to Canada's Atlantic coast, sea otters to the Pacific, and beaver pelts to the interior. For centuries, fishing and trapping were Canada's most important industries, and even today they provide a way of life for thousands across the country.

Off Atlantic Canada, Nova Scotians drag Georges Bank for scallops, while Newfoundlanders trawl the Grand Banks for cod. New Brunswickers trap lobsters and Quebeckers from the Gaspé seine herring, while Prince Edward Islanders nurse Malpeque oysters or comb the sea for giant bluefin tuna.

In the Pacific, British Columbia's

A purse seiner sets out from Vancouver to catch herring off the Pacific coast.

fishermen troll for salmon or seine herring and halibut. In the interior, fishing tugs and skiffs net freshwater species like whitefish and lake trout. In the north, Inuit catch arctic char and hunt sea mammals like seal, walrus, and beluga whales, while Yukoners net salmon in fish wheels.

Before 1977, Canada's offshore fish stocks were declining rapidly through overfishing by other nations. Then Canada declared a fisheries zone extending 200 nautical miles (about 370 km) from land. Only licensed vessels may fish within the zones, fish stocks have recovered, and Canada's fishing industry is booming again.

The trapping industry faced its most serious crisis in the 1930s, when in many areas beaver and other furbearers were faced with extinction. Several provinces created special reserves to allow the animals to recover, and introduced registered traplines that limited the number of active trappers.

Today, fur has become valuable enough for professional trappers to make a respectable living. Fashions change, and there may be sudden demand for short-haired or long-haired pelts or for individual species like lynx and arctic fox. The important thing is that the furbearers themselves seem able to meet the demand.

AGRICULTURE

On Canada's prairies, Texas meets the Ukraine. Cattlemen neighbour grain farmers, and in many instances it makes sense to raise crops and livestock together. Grain is fed to the cattle to fatten them for slaughter.

In Atlantic Canada, the potato is king. Seed and processing potatoes are grown on Prince Edward Island and in the St. John river valley of New Brunswick. Nova Scotia's Annapolis valley grows apples, and the Chebucto peninsula produces blueberries. Newfoundlanders have little arable land, but do raise livestock and vegetables.

In every province there are dairy farms, most of all in Quebec. There, herds of Holsteins and Ayrshires thrive on fodder and oats grown locally, and on waste from the sugar beet industry. An important Quebec specialty is maple syrup, tree sap tapped in spring and boiled in vats to dispose of most of its water content.

Ontario has more farms than any other province, and they produce a greater range of products. Vineyards, tobacco farms, sheep farms, turkey farms — the great cities of Eastern Canada are within easy range, and Ontario's farmers take advantage of them.

Fall is round-up time in southern Alberta and Saskatchewan. Growing steers are separated from their mothers and may be sold to a feedlot for finishing.

Clear skies provide ideal conditions for
Saskatchewan's grain harvest, as a swather
cuts the wheat and lays it on the stubble
to dry.

Beef, corn, hogs, and fruit from Ontario
serve markets across half of Canada.

West of the Rockies, British Columbia is Canada's largest apple producer.
There are dairy farms in the Fraser valley
and beef ranches in the Cariboo, and
wheat is grown in the Peace river country of the north. Vancouver Island's
climate gives it a head start on the
growing season, and its spring flowers
are in demand all over Canada.

Cities are served by the farms on
their doorsteps, but the prairie heartland
serves the world. The grain of Alberta,
Saskatchewan, and Manitoba is exported to countries east, west, and
south, and western beef is eaten all over
Canada. Improving technology means
that the prairie provinces are more productive than ever.

The size and scope of Canada's
farms vary greatly even within regions. A
mechanized grain farm in Saskatchewan
may cover 500 ha or more yet is worked

Vineyards in southern British Columbia
and south-western Ontario produce the
grapes used to make Canadian wine.

by a single family. A specialized fruit
farm in Ontario's Niagara peninsula
may cover only a few hectares, yet
requires a large labour force.

Honey from the Peace river district,
raspberries from the Fraser valley,
pumpkins from southern Ontario, sheep
from Cape Breton Island — all these
products must find markets whether inside Canada or beyond. Aiding the
farmers are elaborate marketing ar-

rangements that make their job much
easier.

The most famous marketing scheme
is run by the Canadian Wheat Board,
the federal agency that is alone responsible for wheat, oats, and barley exported from Western Canada and intended for human consumption. Provincial marketing boards may control the
sale of products like milk, eggs, poultry,
or fruit.

THE FORESTS

Nobody can ever hope to guess how many trees there are in Canada, but it would be no surprise if the number ran into trillions. All the provinces and both territories have significant forest resources, and they are the raw materials of Canada's most valuable exports.

In British Columbia, loggers fall Douglas firs destined for giant sawmills on the coast. In Manitoba, large areas of the boreal forest are clearcut to feed the mill complex at The Pas. Newfoundlanders and Quebeckers produce

newsprint, Saskatchewan makes particleboard, and even Prince Edward Islanders saw lumber.

In the past, forest industries tended to be divided into two groups — those making lumber, and those making pulp and paper. Now they are more likely to be integrated, but it is helpful to distinguish between three main stages in their operations.

The first stage is the work in the woods. Timber cruisers decide which wood is to be cut, taking care not to remove more of it than the forest can replace. Logging crews use chainsaws or

Traditionally, Canada's forest industries have used water to float logs to their mills. At a wet sorting yard in British Columbia, boom 'dozers' nudge logs into their proper places.

sophisticated harvesting machines to fell the trees, and then buck (trim) and stack them ready for the mill.

In the old days loggers tended to remove particular trees from forest stands and leave the others standing. Today, they are more likely to cut down all the trees in a specific stand, leaving a large hole in the forest that can be replanted with selected seedlings of a particular species.

Increasingly, forestry is becoming a type of agriculture. Foresters manage their trees as a farmer tends his crops. They protect the trees against disease and insect pests, they thin their stands to allow healthy trees more room to grow, and they are on constant watch for fire that must be extinguished from the air or on the ground.

When logs reach the mill, they enter the forest industries' second stage. When possible, the best logs are reserved for sawmills and plywood mills, where they are spun on a lathe to produce a thin veneer. Undersize and defective logs will probably be pulped, their fibres separated by grinding or by cooking them in chemicals.

Most of Canada's lumber and

Sophisticated machinery has kept Canada's forest industries profitable. Here in New Brunswick, a delimbing machine strips a log of its branches.

plywood is consumed domestically or in the United States. Most of the wood pulp — nearly 70 per cent — is processed into paper in Canada. There is enough left over to make Canada the world's leading exporter of wood pulp, and as a producer it is second only to the United States.

The third stage of forest processing is manufacturing. Some industries turn lumber into boxes, barrels, and a host of other items from doors to prefabricated buildings. Wood pulp is used by Canada's many papermills, most of which specialize in newsprint and kraft and packaging paper.

In spite of rising competition in outside markets, Canada still produces nearly 40 per cent of the world's newsprint. Nearly all of it is exported. Most of the newsprint mills are in Ontario and Quebec, and there are several more in the Atlantic provinces. Kraft paper production is increasing steadily, particularly in the interior of British Columbia.

The outside competition has forced Canada's forest industries to improve their efficiency. New machines have cut down on labour requirements, the forests themselves are being managed

under strict controls, and logging crews are travelling far afield in search of new forest areas to exploit.

In view of these developments, provincial governments are forcing forest producers to take care of the environment. Forests are much more than reservoirs of trees. They shelter wildlife, they influence water resources, they serve recreational needs, and above all, they provide most of Canada's oxygen.

One possibility that has been broached only tentatively is the use of forests to provide energy. Forest industries regularly use 'hog fuel' — their own waste products — to generate electricity. There is no reason why vast, swiftly growing plantations should not provide energy enough for all of Canada's population.

Quebec is Canada's leading producer of pulp and paper. This is a newsprint mill within the James Bay region.

Hidden in Alberta's northern forest, a drilling rig probes deep sediments in search of oil and natural gas.

Some mines are underground, some are worked from the surface. This is the great Cyprus Anvil lead-zinc mine in the Yukon, the mainstay of the territory's economy.

MINERALS

Gold in the territories, potash in Saskatchewan, zinc in New Brunswick, coal in Cape Breton — the list of Canada's mineral resources is long and impressive. Of the world's major metals, only aluminum is missing from Canada's inventory, and the country makes a clean sweep of the important fuels and industrial materials.

There are mines in every province except Prince Edward Island, and mining is the principal industry in both the Yukon and Northwest Territories. By value of production, Alberta's oil and natural gas give it an edge over other provinces, but Ontario's base metals mines make it the mining industry's largest employer.

Ontario produces most of Canada's precious metals too — gold from hard rock mines in the Precambrian Shield, silver recovered as a by-product of nickel mined from Sudbury. There are gold and silver mines in the Northwest Territories as well, and placer miners still wash gold from the creeks of the Yukon and British Columbia.

Iron ore is Canada's premier base metal, nearly all of it from Labrador, Quebec, and Ontario. Nickel is mined at Sudbury and in northern Manitoba. British Columbia ranks first in copper production, followed by Ontario and Quebec, while Ontario leads in zinc and British Columbia in lead and molybdenum.

Uranium, cobalt, tin, tungsten, titanium — all these metals and many more have their special uses, and all are found in Canada. Most of them are smelted and refined domestically as well, though much of British Columbia's base metals production is exported as ore concentrate.

Asbestos, potash, and salt are Canada's most valuable non-metallic minerals. Most of the asbestos comes from southern Quebec, and makes Canada the world's leading producer. Saskatchewan holds immense reserves of potash, and there is more in New Brunswick. Salt and gypsum are mined in Ontario and Nova Scotia.

Until quite recently, Nova Scotia was Canada's leading producer of coal. Now it has been overshadowed by British Columbia and Alberta, both exporting to Japan. As the price of oil climbs higher, coal becomes more attractive within Canada itself and is being used to generate electricity.

Coal is a hydrocarbon, a fossil fuel like oil and natural gas. Alberta has been Canada's leading petroleum producer since the 1940s, and holds immense

Energy

One of Canada's greatest advantages is an abundance of energy sources. The rivers provide hydro power, uranium mines feed nuclear generating stations, and the country is all but self-sufficient in fossil fuels. Alternative energy sources like wood, wind, and the sun have been virtually ignored.

Counting all forms of primary energy, oil and natural gas produce more than 60 per cent of the total. Oil fuels vehicles, heats buildings, runs factories, and performs many other tasks. Until recently, gas seemed much less versatile, but the rising price of oil has persuaded consumers of all kinds to take gas more seriously.

Nearly all of Canada's oil and natural gas comes from the western provinces, and is piped west, south, and east as far as Ontario and western Quebec. Much of Eastern Canada's oil has been imported, but that may change, and the gas pipeline system is to be extended to reach the Maritimes. Newfoundland alone will be remote from the system.

Both oil and natural gas are used to fire electrical generating stations, and increasingly so is coal. In many provinces, such stations are kept in reserve to boost regular electrical supplies generated from water. Manitoba, Saskatchewan, British Columbia, Ontario, and Quebec all have impressive hydro capacity.

Lack of hydro makes electricity expensive in Nova Scotia and in Prince

Nuclear power stations like Ontario's Pickering use the Canadian-designed CANDU reactor system.

Edward Island, which receives power from New Brunswick by way of a submarine cable. A similar cable connects Vancouver Island with the mainland, and another will be laid to transmit Labrador power to the people of Newfoundland.

Ontario has three nuclear generating stations, all using the Candu heavy water system developed in Canada. There are other such stations in Quebec and New Brunswick, but the remaining provinces have said they prefer to seek out alternative energy sources rather than take risks with radioactive materials.

reserves of fossil fuels tied up in the Athabasca oil sands. Saskatchewan has oil too, and so have Manitoba, British Columbia, and the Northwest Territories.

Natural gas is proving more valuable than oil, whether as a heating fuel or as the raw material of the petrochemical industry. The gasfields overlap Western Canada's oilfields, and the gas they produce is piped to points east, west, and south. The pipeline system is to be extended to cover all Southern Canada.

Deep under Saskatchewan, miners service a continuous boring machine that tunnels through thick beds of potash.

MANUFACTURING

Mining, agriculture, and other primary industries produce the raw materials. The manufacturing sector adds value to them through processing. In Canada, the largest single sector in the manufacturing field is the food and beverage processing industry.

Fish packing plants, flour mills, breweries, fruit canneries, candy factories — all told, some 5000 separate plants are included in the sector. They employ roughly 17 per cent of the total labour force, and produce about 90 per cent of all the processed food consumed in Canada as well as a surplus for export.

The food and beverages sector is spread evenly across the country, and so is the forest products industry. There are sawmills in every province and both territories, and pulp and paper producers in every province except Prince Edward Island. Other forest products include plywood (especially in B.C.) and wood panels.

Like the forest products industries, Canada's iron and steel industry is based on an immense supply of raw materials. Much of the iron ore mined in Canada is exported as concentrate, but large quantities go to integrated steelmills in Ontario and Nova Scotia. In addition, mills across Canada make steel from scrap metal.

Canada's shipbuilding industry was a world leader in the nineteenth century, and still flourishes today through yards like this one in Saint John, New Brunswick.

Copper, lead, zinc, and nickel are all smelted and refined in Canada, and so is alumina, imported from the Caribbean and elsewhere. All these metals serve as the raw materials of supplementary manufacturers, among them those that produce transportation equipment.

Ships are built in Nova Scotia, New Brunswick, Quebec, and Ontario (and British Columbia too, though from imported steel). Automobiles are assembled in the eastern provinces, tank trucks in Saskatchewan, heavy duty trucks in British Columbia, railcars and locomotives in Quebec. Aircraft are built both in Ontario and Quebec.

All these industries rely on improving technology to keep abreast of their rivals. So do electronics manufacturers. There are more than 700 companies in Canada making electronics products, which range from television sets to telephones, from computers to control systems.

The electronics industry is not to be confused with the electrical products industry. Batteries, generating equip-

Among manufacturing industries, food and beverage processing is Canada's leading employer. This is a freshwater fish packing plant in Winnipeg.

ment, switches, transformers, motors, bulbs, and appliances all count as electrical products, and at least 90 per cent of the plants that make them are in Quebec and Ontario.

One sector even more closely associated with Quebec is textiles and clothing manufacturing. In many cases the finished products of one plant serve as the raw materials of another. Some of them make synthetic yarn from chemicals, some transform synthetic or natural yarn into fabrics, some cut fabric and sew garments.

Footwear, furniture, tobacco products, rubber, plastics, printing, publishing, metal fabricating, machinery, chemicals — the manufacturing field seems to know no bounds. One sector that is developing rapidly is petrochemicals manufacturing, chiefly in Eastern Canada, but increasingly in Alberta as well.

Hamilton, Ontario, is the home of Canada's two major steel producers. Here, molten steel is being poured into a succession of ingot molds.

Construction

The entire manufacturing sector accounts for about one-quarter of Canada's gross national product, the value of all goods and services produced. That compares with roughly four per cent for mining, three per cent for agriculture, and six per cent for construction.

Construction, in fact, is the largest single goods-producing industry in the country. Roughly 100 000 contracting firms employ about seven per cent of the total labour force, and the industry also provides work for firms of architects, materials suppliers, and many other companies.

Construction firms fall into three main categories. Some specialize in residential construction, which amounts to nearly 20 per cent of the industry. Some work on non-residential projects (about 55 per cent) like hospitals and factories. The remainder are engineering firms.

Since 1960 there have been major changes in the construction industry. Before, most contractors had to halt their operations over the winter. To-

day, improved materials and new techniques help them to function all through the year. That makes the industry more stable and offsets the rising costs of labour and materials.

The leading clients of the construction industry are the various levels of government. Their direct expenditure on various projects pays for about

one-third of all construction activity. Besides, their programs have major indirect influence on a further 20 per cent or even more.

A contracting firm erects a store complex in Ottawa. Construction is Canada's most valuable goods-producing industry.

TRADE AND COMMERCE

Canadian producers supply roughly 70 per cent of all the goods consumed in Canada, but the remainder are imported. To pay for them, Canadians export nearly one-quarter of what they produce — some goods in their raw state, some partially processed, and some of them manufactured end products.

Canada's leading trade partner is the United States. The North American neighbours do more business together than any other two nations in the world. In recent years, roughly 70 per cent of Canada's imports have originated there.

Softwood lumber for construction, newsprint, iron ore, nickel, asbestos, potash, fish, petroleum — the list of Canada's exports to the United States is long and varied. In return, Canada receives food products and many manufactured goods, among them appliances, automobiles, and specialized machinery.

In most cases, imports and exports are liable to the duties and excise taxes imposed in the two countries. Sometimes the duties are designed to protect specific industries. An exception is made for agricultural equipment, which has had free access across the international border since the 1940s.

Another special case is the import and export of automobiles and auto parts. In 1965 Canada and the United States signed a special pact under which

Economic power has been shifting from Eastern Canada to the west, and in particular to Calgary as the focus of Canada's oil and natural gas industry.

'original manufacturers' in the two countries can import and export auto products duty free. A manufacturer can mass produce for all North America from a single location.

The auto pact has its critics, for some feel that it has lost Canada more than it has gained. However, many industrialists believe that it will be copied in other fields of industry. Meanwhile, Canada develops new trading ties with other partners, notably those of the European Economic Community.

Before 1973, the EEC was not one of Canada's major trading partners. It consisted of only six countries — West Germany, France, the Netherlands, Belgium, and Luxembourg. Then three more joined — Ireland, Denmark, and most significantly Britain, one of Canada's closest partners for longer than two centuries.

Today, the EEC takes 12 per cent of Canada's total exports, amounting to nearly 40 per cent of its exports outside the United States. Most of these exports are raw materials such as cereals, forest products, and minerals. In return, the

Some consumer goods must be imported, but Canada produces most of its own requirements. Full advantage is taken of Ontario's agricultural season to grow fresh fruit and vegetables.

The Labour Force

By the late 1970s, roughly ten million Canadians were counted as belonging to the work force. The figure included employers and employees, the self-employed, and about one million would-be workers who at any one time were without jobs.

With government encouragement, industries across the country were working hard to create new jobs. However, the work force was growing even as the jobs became available. Young people were leaving school and college to join the work force, and housewives were abandoning their kitchen stoves to lead a more fulfilling life.

Roughly one-third of all members of the work force belonged to trade unions, which exist to provide their members with bargaining power. In all, there are about 12 000 union locals in Canada, which together belong to some 600 separate trade unions. Some of the unions are national, some international, and some independent.

The largest union in Canada is CUPE, the Canadian Union of Public Employees, with about 200 000 members. The second largest is the Canadian section of an international union, the United Steelworkers of America.

The smallest unions have fewer than 100 members, but the average membership is between 10 000 and 50 000.

Most, but not all, unions belong to one of four central labour foundations that give their members lobbying power. By far the largest is the Canadian Labour Congress (CLC), which accounts for nearly 70 per cent of all Canada's union members. The second largest is the Confederation of National Trade Unions, almost entirely within Quebec.

One of the CLC's chief purposes is

Labour conflicts have cost Canada heavily in wasted time and lost earnings. Here, provincial labour conciliators in Toronto persuade employers and union representatives to discuss their differences.

to serve as a lobbying group, bringing labour matters to the attention of the national government. The CLC charters ten provincial labour federations that serve the same function in the provinces. The provincial federations charter local labour councils that lobby municipalities.

EEC provides roughly ten per cent of all Canada's imports, mostly manufactured goods.

Canada's third biggest trading partner is Japan, which imports large amounts of Canadian coal, base metals, and forest products. Japan's exports to Canada are mainly manufactured goods, most of them involving sophisticated technology. Other parts of South-East Asia export textiles and cheap clothing, while China imports wheat.

Latin America, Australia, New Zealand, and Southern Africa figure among Canada's trading partners. Individual provinces develop trade ties of their own and often Canada's far-flung regions must trade with each other as nations do.

Vancouver has become the leading port of North America's Pacific coast. Much of the traffic it handles is Canadian-produced grain and minerals destined for the orient.

SURFACE TRANSPORT

The aim of a transportation system is to carry passengers or cargoes to their destinations as speedily and efficiently as possible. Canada's immense distances have posed great challenges for transport engineers, but there seems to be no limit to their ingenuity.

Haida war canoes on the Pacific, Inuit dog teams in the arctic, Red river carts on the prairies, square-rigged cargo ships in the Maritimes — each mode of transport has reflected contemporary needs and technology. When it is no longer needed or has been improved on, it is abandoned, and society remembers it only as a passing curiosity.

Flat-bottomed York boats served the fur trade from Hudson Bay to the Rockies. Stagecoaches carried the mails across the prairies, and horse-drawn carioles raced across the snow-covered fields of rural Quebec. Sternwheelers cruised the Yukon river, while coal-fired locomotives puffed across northern Ontario.

Today, giant eighteen-wheeler trucks roar down the broad highways that cross Canada from coast to coast. A dozen locomotives are coupled to bulk trains that are more than two kilometres long. Specially designed 'lakers' squeeze into locks on the St. Lawrence seaway, and natural gas speeds east through underground pipelines.

Of course, many of the innovations in transport come from outside Canada, but an impressive number originated locally. One of the most inspired has been the snowmobile, invented in the 1920s by J. A. Bombardier of Quebec. The snowmobile has been manufactured commercially since the 1950s, and is in use all over the country.

An even more important invention stems from the Yukon, which relies on a rail link between Whitehorse and Skagway on the coast of Alaska. To cut down on breakage and pilfering of cargoes shipped from Vancouver, in 1950 the White Pass and Yukon Route railroad began packing them in sealed containers.

The containers were built to standard dimensions, so could be quickly transferred from ship to shore or from train to truck. The railroad ordered ships especially designed for containers, and pioneered a concept that has since been adopted worldwide. Container traffic has become commonplace ashore, afloat, and in the air.

Inland container depots in Winnipeg, Toronto, and other centres load and unload container trains made up of flatbed cars. The trains serve container terminals on the coast — particularly those in Vancouver, Halifax, and Saint John. Container ships bound for other ports visit these terminals on a regular schedule.

Of course, container traffic is only one facet of operations at Canada's ports. A certain amount of general cargo is handled as in the old days, as well as

The Trans-Canada Highway traverses the boreal forest of eastern Manitoba on its way from coast to coast.

Heavy trucks have proved their worth in forest operations and many other industries. Here, a truck hauls logs across a canyon in British Columbia's interior.

'Laker' ships like this one are designed to fit the locks of the St. Lawrence Seaway, which extends from the Great Lakes to Montreal and beyond.

specialized goods like automobiles. A major part of each port's work is the handling of bulk cargoes — wheat, potash, ore concentrate, coal, and much besides.

Canada used to have a major deepsea fleet manned by Canadians. Today, most deepsea ships owned by Canadians have foreign crews and are registered elsewhere. Canadian seaman are better represented on coastal ships and on the bulk lakers that navigate the St. Lawrence seaway and the Great Lakes.

Opened in 1959, the seaway allows deepsea ships to travel between the Gulf of St. Lawrence and the far west of Lake Superior. It is closed by ice for about four months of the year — in contrast with the navigation season on Hudson Bay, which is open for only four months. There, ships visit the Manitoba port of Churchill.

Most of Canada's railroads follow routes that were laid out long before World War I, but there similarities end. They carry many fewer passengers and much more freight than in the old days, and computers can pinpoint the position of each individual car. Gradually the rail system is being extended in Canada's north.

The railroads' great rival is the highway system, a phenomenon of the twentieth century that may soon decline. Rising gasoline prices are making it far less attractive to haul freight by road or even to drive automobiles for long distances. Travellers are being urged to use public transport while haulers consign goods to the railroads.

An important part of the highway system is the network of ferries that links Canada's islands with the mainland. Vancouver Island is connected with Vancouver, Prince Edward Island with New Brunswick and Nova Scotia, and Newfoundland with Cape Breton and Labrador. Cape Breton is attached to mainland Nova Scotia by a causeway.

Locomotive overhaul in Canadian National's repair shops in Moncton, New Brunswick. Canadian National and CP Rail operate services throughout Canada.

AVIATION

The twentieth century has seen Canadian aviation advance from being the plaything of pioneers to become carrier of the nation. Today, Canadians fly upwards of 21 500 machines that range from tiny floatplanes to giant jetliners that span the continent in fewer than six hours.

The first powered flight in Canada was made by J. A. D. McCurdy of Cape Breton in 1909. McCurdy was a member of the Aerial Experiment As-

sociation founded by Alexander Graham Bell at Baddeck, Cape Breton. Each member of the association designed his own machine, and McCurdy's *Silver Dart* was first into the air.

Many young Canadians learned how to fly during World War I. When it was over, many of them wanted to develop commercial aviation at home. The government was not enthusiastic, for there was a railroad crisis. Too many routes were competing for too little traffic, and scheduled flights between cities could only make things worse.

Light aircraft have played a major role in opening Canada's northland, but the dog teams made famous by explorers, Mounties, and trappers have been eclipsed by snowmobiles.

Instead, the pilots looked northwards. Prospectors were at work in the bush, and there were new mines to be developed. Flying by the seat of their pants, the bush pilots ferried men and equipment to remote locations far from civilization, and opened the way to development of the north.

By the 1930s many communities had airfields of their own. One was Edmonton's Blatchford Field, today the oldest airport in Canada. During the depression years the federal government systematically built new airports and upgraded existing ones, ready for the launching of scheduled services across the country.

To operate these services, the government formed Trans-Canada Air Lines (TCA), the forerunner of Air Canada. TCA made its first flights in 1937, and within a year was operating from Vancouver to Montreal. By 1940 there were services to the Maritimes, and by 1941 there were services to New York.

Air Canada jets display the national carrier's familiar livery at airports throughout North America, Europe, and elsewhere.

During World War II, pilots from a score of countries were trained at bases in Canada. Many were Canadian, and the experience they gained in Europe and elsewhere proved invaluable when the war was over. Flying the Atlantic had become commonplace, and dozens of new airports and airfields were in operation.

Trans-Canada Air Lines emerged from the war with a rival. For years there had been a number of small flying companies operating local services. In 1942 the Canadian Pacific Railway bought ten of the largest and combined them as a single company, Canadian Pacific Airlines.

At first, CP Air served outlying areas, feeding the national services provided by TCA. Gradually the newcomers acquired new aircraft and went into competition. At last the federal government was obliged to intervene, and ever since has divided the world (and Canada) between the two airlines.

Today, Air Canada has its headquarters in Montreal and CP Air in Vancouver. CP Air's domestic services cover British Columbia, Alaska, and the Yukon, and also Winnipeg, Toronto, and Montreal. Air Canada's mandate is to serve all Canada except the northwest, but in practice the airline concentrates on the cities of the south.

Air Canada's international services take it to many cities of the United States, the Caribbean, and northern Europe. CP Air flies to the Far East, Australasia, Latin America, and southern Europe. Several other Canadian operators, notably Wardair of Edmonton and Quebecair of Montreal, also fly to international destinations.

Within Canada, the two 'mainline' carriers are complemented by five smaller airlines known as regional carriers. Pacific Western serves British Columbia and western Alberta; Transair the rest of the prairies and north-western Ontario; Nordair the remainder of Ontario and north-western Quebec.

Quebecair serves Quebec east of Montreal; Eastern Provincial caters to the Atlantic region. There is some overlapping between regions — Transair

Empress of Canada, **a Boeing 747, is part of CP Air's international fleet. The airline flies to the orient, Australasia, South America, and Europe.**

may fly to Toronto and Eastern Provincial to Montreal. Besides their southern operations, Pacific Western, Transair, and Nordair all serve points north of the 60th parallel.

Separate from the regional carriers is the bewildering world of 'general aviation,' smaller aircraft with a multitude of purposes whether commercial or private. Charter operators carry tourists on

High above Lake Ontario, a De Havilland Dash-7 built in Toronto shows off the potential of STOL (short take-off and landing) aircraft.

a fishing trip; Toronto businessmen commute in an executive jet; prairie skydivers hurtle into space from an aircraft — general aviation's versatility has made it an essential feature of Canadian life.

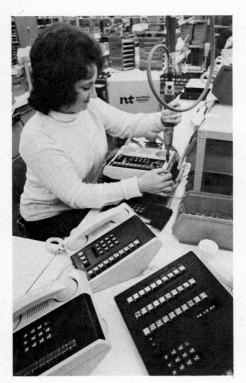

The telephone was a Canadian invention, in that Alexander Graham Bell first outlined the principle of 'electronic speech' in Brantford, Ontario.

TELECOMMUNICATIONS

Anik satellites project colour television to Canada's arctic, and telephone subscribers dial direct to almost all parts of North America and other continents too. Telecommunications have come a long way since Canada's first telegraph went into operation in 1846.

Telecommunication means any transmission or reception of words, images, or data of whatever sort, by means of electronic signals. 'Tele' means 'far,' so is easily compounded with other Greek expressions like 'graph' (write) and 'phone' (sound) or a Latin-based word like 'vision.'

Telegraph, the system that began it all, was invented by an American, Samuel Morse, in the 1830s. Not until 1845 was it available commercially, but in the next year Canada's first line was erected between Hamilton and Toronto. By the 1850s, there were telegraph lines all the way to Halifax.

In the 1860s a bold entrepreneur persuaded backers to finance an overland telegraph from North America to Europe by way of Russia. It was to pass through British Columbia and what is now the Yukon, and line crews began cutting into the forest. By 1866 the line stretched 1360 km through B.C. when the project was halted by bad news.

The news was of a cable laid under the Atlantic. After several previous failures, the steamer *Great Eastern* had delivered the cable to Heart's Content in eastern Newfoundland. The cable was an instant success, and for decades Heart's Content would serve as the most important link between North America and Europe.

The 1870s saw the building of telegraph lines all across Canada, and a remarkable invention in Brantford, Ontario. There in 1874 Alexander Graham Bell told his father of his new concept, electronic speech. Bell worked on the idea in Massachusetts and in 1876 patented it as the telephone.

Bell's early experiments were re-

Toronto's CN telecommunications transmission tower (right) dwarfs the highrise office blocks of the downtown core.

stricted to neighbouring rooms. To show his telephone worked over longer distances, Bell took his equipment to Brantford. He persuaded a local telegraph manager to let him use a line, and set up a transmitter and receiver several kilometres apart.

The experiments were conducted, and the telephone was a success. Soon telephones were being manufactured in both the United States and Canada, where Bell gave his father rights to his patent. Before long there were local telephone systems in most cities of Eastern Canada.

It was to be many years before the telephone overtook the telegraph. Meanwhile, the Italian inventor Guglielmo Marconi arrived in Newfoundland in 1901 to test his discovery of 'wireless' radio transmissions. On Signal Hill in St. John's, Marconi picked up a signal sent from an assistant of his in England.

Marconi had learned to control radio waves in 1894, and used them to communicate with ships at sea. Now he was ready to transmit across oceans. He set up a permanent transmitting station, not in Newfoundland, but on Cape Breton. There at Glace Bay he laid the foundations of all 'wireless' telecommunications today.

From World War I, telecommunications strengthened its hold on Canadian life. There were several *thousand* separate telephone subscriber systems across the country — nowhere more than in Saskatchewan, where in 1921 there were 1200. Soon radio broadcasting spread like wildfire, and television was introduced in the 1950s.

Today, Canadian telecommunications uses a national grid of electronic 'highways' — land wires, underground cables, high frequency radio links, microwave networks, and Anik domestic satellites. Each 'highway' links a transmitting terminal — say a telephone or telex — with a receiving terminal at the other end.

The backbone of the system is the chain of line-of-sight microwave towers that spans Canada. The towers receive radio signals, strengthen them, and retransmit them to the next tower along, usually about 45 km away. Canada's three Anik ('brother') satellites are microwave repeaters in the sky.

The Media

Among the best customers of the telecommunications industry are the media, particularly newspapers and radio and television stations. Daily newspapers began using 'wire services' in the early days of the telegraph, and telegraphers often served as local news correspondents.

Today, there are roughly 115 daily newspapers in Canada, many of them members of large chains. More than 30 of them, mostly serving small cities, are part of the Thomson newspaper empire. The Southam group owns large dailies in Vancouver, Calgary, Edmonton, Winnipeg, Hamilton, Ottawa, and Montreal.

Commercial radio in Canada started with station XWA (now CFCF) of Montreal, which went on the air in 1919. Today there are commercial

A television special is rehearsed at the Canadian Broadcasting Corporation studios in Toronto.

stations over most of Canada, licensed to serve particular regions. In addition there are the non-commercial, publicly owned networks operated by the Canadian Broadcasting Corporation (CBC) and its French arm, Radio-Canada, which had their origins in 1932.

Canadian television broadcasting began in 1952, when the CBC began transmitting in Toronto and Montreal. Today, the CBC and Radio-Canada provide programming for stations all across Canada, some controlled by them and some affiliated. CBC's rivals include the CTV and Global networks, which have their headquarters in Toronto, and Télé-Metropole in Quebec.

THE CANADIANS

There are Canadians who dress in kilts and play bagpipes, and other Canadians who ride bucking bulls at rodeos. Chinese Canadians celebrate New Year with a dragon dance, Ukrainian Canadians exchange decorated eggs at Easter, and Caribbean Canadians play cricket on sports fields in Toronto.

All these activities are aspects of Canada's cultural mosaic, which is very different from the 'melting pot' tradition of the United States. In Canada, some ethnic groups have managed to keep their traditions alive for centuries at a stretch, and they encourage new immigrants to take pride in all that they stand for.

In Nova Scotia, the Germans of Lunenburg have been established since the 1750s. In New Brunswick, the Acadians are proud to be separate from the French of Quebec. In Manitoba, Icelanders of the Interlake region used to have their own republic. In each case, the community is proud of what it is and is also proud to be Canadian.

According to Statistics Canada's census of 1971, only 85 per cent of Canadian residents had been born in Canada. The remainder — many of them naturalized citizens — had come from scores of countries around the world. There was a bias towards those from Western Europe, particularly Britain and Italy.

The census also analyzed the ethnic backgrounds of Canadians. Nearly half (44.6 per cent) were of British ancestry, more than one-quarter (28 per cent) were of French descent. Sadly, the British were not listed as English, Scottish, Irish, and Welsh, for there are big differences. Many suspect that Scottish Canadians hold a considerable lead over the English, and perhaps even over the French.

Of course, several other major influences were listed in the census. The largest appeared to be German (6.1 per cent), Italian (3.4 per cent), Ukrainian (2.7 per cent), Dutch (2 per cent), and

A busy afternoon in Ottawa as thousands converge on Parliament Hill to celebrate Canada's birthday, July 1.

Scandinavian (1.8 per cent). Indians and Inuit amounted to no more than 1.4 per cent.

The most visible aspects of a culture are its special foods, costumes, songs, and dances. Those are the main ingredients of the many cultural festivals held across Canada. Among them are the German Oktoberfest in Kitchener, Ontario, and the National Ukrainian Festival in Dauphin, Manitoba.

The largest ethnic festivals, however, are in Winnipeg and Toronto. Both cities go en fête for a week each summer, with upwards of 30 pavilions organized by ethnic groups in the names of cities of the world. Visitors gain access by passport, and a single evening can take them to four 'countries' or even more.

Since the early 1970s, multiculturalism has been official government policy in Canada. Immigrants are urged to integrate with the English and French communities (or better still, both), but are told that integration is not the same as assimilation. If they can keep their own culture alive, so much the better.

Most of the new arrivals are given 'landed immigrant' status, which means the right to permanent residence in Canada. After three years of residence they can apply for Canadian citizenship, regarded as one of the world's most far-ranging as it embraces so many different cultures.

East Indians born in Bombay, West Indians born in Jamaica, Canadian Indians born in the Yukon — all are counted among Canada's citizens. Landed immigrants wanting to acquire the status through naturalization are called for examination by a citizenship court to decide if they qualify.

The citizenship judge has to determine if the applicant has an adequate knowledge of English or French, of Canada, and of the rights and duties of Canadian citizenship. If the applicant is passed, he is invited to a public ceremony in which he takes Canada's oath or affirmation of allegiance and finally receives his papers.

Canada's Scottish tradition is as strong as the French heritage so prominent in Quebec. Here, pipers parade at Ingonish on Cape Breton Island.

First Peoples

Two elements of Canada's cultural mosaic have special status. One is the Indian population, nearly 280 000 strong and scattered all over Canada. The other is the Inuit world, approaching 20 000 people located in the Northwest Territories, northern Quebec, and Labrador.

Under a proclamation of George III made in 1763, Canada's native peoples may not be deprived of their land without their consent. That is the background to the many land treaties signed between Indians and the Canadian government during the nineteenth century, and to land claim negotiations that continue today.

About 70 per cent of Indians live in communities known as bands, some of them nomadic but most settled on reserves set aside for them by the federal government. Many live by hunting, fishing, and trapping like their ancestors. Some have organized their own businesses, for instance sawmills and handcrafts co-operatives.

All registered Indians are citizens of Canada, so have the same privileges and duties as other citizens. They can vote in federal and provincial elections, but they must obey the law like everyone else. As Indians, they have certain additional privileges, not least

Indians, Inuit, French, and British were Canada's founding peoples. In Cambridge Bay in the high arctic, an Inuit mother shows her baby to an admiring nurse.

freedom from property taxes.

Nearly all the Inuit live in small 'hamlets' on the coast of Hudson Bay and the polar sea. A number of them have become famous for the sculptures and prints that they produce, but Inuit themselves place greater value on human resourcefulness and stamina that they have inherited from their forbears.

TEN PROVINCES

In law, Quebec and Prince Edward Island have equal status. Both are provinces of Canada with their constitutional powers set out in the British North America Act. Both are administered in the name of the Crown, with the monarch represented by provincial lieutenant-governors.

In practice, of course, there are major imbalances between the two. The whole of Prince Edward Island is barely one-tenth the size of Saguenay, a single provincial park in Quebec. Quebeckers outnumber Islanders by more than 50 to one, and the complete Island population would fit comfortably into Montreal's southern suburbs.

Imbalances like these bother some authorities on Canada's constitution. These authorities would like to see the provinces reorganized in five great regions — Pacific, Prairie, Ontario, Quebec, and Atlantic — with a sixth covering the north. They feel the gain in efficiency would more than compensate for any loss of history and heritage.

Significantly, most of those who hold these views are in Quebec and Ontario. Atlantic Canadians and prairie-dwellers seem much less enthusiastic, for each province in their regions has its own traditions and its own way of doing things. Often the traditions are directly contrary to those of neighbouring provinces.

Take Alberta and Saskatchewan, 'twins' in that both became provinces in 1905 yet otherwise quite different. Alberta has a tradition of free enterprise, a preference cultivated by successive provincial governments. Saskatchewanians, however, take more interest in co-operating with each other for the benefit of society as a whole.

There are big differences, too, between Nova Scotia and New Brunswick. Nova Scotia is truly maritime, connected with the rest of the country by a narrow isthmus so that the sea penetrates every aspect of its life. In comparison, New Brunswick is continental, for the sea's influence affects no more than the coastline.

Even the smallest of Canada's provinces are the size of whole countries elsewhere in the world. Besides, each of them is split into distinct regions. Cape Breton Island has more in common with Newfoundland and Prince Edward Island than with mainland Nova Scotia. Northern Ontario could qualify as a province in its own right.

In Western Canada, the bald-headed prairie of southern Saskatchewan is totally different from the forested Shield country of the north. In British Columbia, towering mountain ranges separate islands of civilization like the Cariboo ranching country, the orchards of the Okanagan, and the mining towns of the Kootenays.

North of the 60th parallel, Yukoners

Manitoba's legislative building is in the heart of Winnipeg, surrounded by the highrise office towers of the city's downtown core.

are proud of the pioneer traditions that set them apart from those who live in the Northwest Territories. The N.W.T. itself is naturally divided into two huge zones north and south of the treeline, and each has a special lifestyle dictated by the terrain, climate, and history.

As yet, the Yukon and Northwest Territories are not provinces. Instead they form a Canadian empire of the north, ruled jointly by the federal government and territorial governments whose powers are being gradually increased. Their executives are headed not by lieutenant-governors representing the monarch but by commissioners representing Ottawa.

Like provinces, the territories have elected legislatures with the authority to make laws in their areas of jurisdiction. In both cases the legislatures are relatively recent innovations, certainly when compared with provincial legislatures that are descended from colonial forbears much older than the national parliament.

Nova Scotia's legislature, for instance, dates from 1758. Prince Edward Island's was established in 1769, New Brunswick's in the 1780s. As Upper and Lower Canada, Ontario and Quebec were given their own legislatures in

1792 and 1793 respectively. Even British Columbia's legislature had its origins in 1856.

More than once, provincial legislatures have come close to taking their province out of Confederation. It has happened twice in Nova Scotia (1867 and 1886), and in 1878 it happened in British Columbia. A Quebec election of 1976 gave power to the Parti Québécois, which was dedicated to Quebec independence.

Some observers felt that the 1976 result was not so much victory for the Parti Québécois as defeat for the Liberals who had preceded them. Even so, the PQ promised that a referendum would be held in which Quebeckers would be given a say in their future. Opinion polls showed that a majority of Quebeckers wanted to remain in Canada.

Montreal is the world's second largest French-speaking city, made rich by the fur trade and today a bastion of Québécois culture.

Time Zones

North America's pioneer settlers told the time by the sun. Inevitably, noon on the east coast was several hours ahead of noon in the west. That posed problems for the telegraphs and later the railroads that spanned the continent, for there was no such thing as standard time.

Late in the 1870s, the Canadian engineer Sandford Fleming persuaded American and Canadian railroads to adopt a universal system. Fleming's success led to an international conference in Washington in 1884, at which the world's nations agreed to recognize 24 standard time zones that girdled the globe.

Where possible, each nation picked a single time frame. Some countries, of course, were too wide. Canada had to designate no fewer than five zones — Atlantic, Eastern, Central, Mountain, and Pacific. Today the country has seven, for the Yukon and Newfoundland have arrangements of their own.

Six of the seven current zones are an even number of hours behind the universal standard at the zero meridian. Newfoundland, however, is 30 minutes ahead of Atlantic time, out of step with the rest of the continent. Newfoundlanders explain that their time standard reflects high noon on Signal Hill in St. John's.

In several cases, time zone boundaries divide provinces into two parts. During summer, most regions of Canada save daylight by advancing clocks by one hour. Complicating the time warp even further, Saskatchewan and the Yukon prefer to abide by standard time all through the year.

Newfoundland's picturesque outports are governed by the province's eccentric time standard, calculated by the position of the sun relative to Signal Hill in St. John's.

Ottawa's Rideau Canal was built before Canada's parliament buildings were a gleam in Queen Victoria's eye.

In winter Ottawa becomes a miniature Amsterdam as skaters crowd the frozen Rideau Canal.

Rideau Canal

Ottawa's tulip beds remind spring visitors of Amsterdam. So does the capital's special pride, the Rideau Canal, which in winter freezes and becomes an immense skating rink.

Most Canadians know how to skate, but Ottawans make it a way of life. On a sunny weekend, as many as 100 000 skaters may be seen on the eight-kilometre stretch of canal carefully maintained for their benefit. Even on weekdays, public servants and others like to slip out during their lunch hour for a swift expedition on the ice.

The Rideau canal was built by British military engineers in the 1820s. Following the War of 1812, the British needed a route from Montreal to the Great Lakes safe from the threat of attack by the United States. The canal's route linked the Ottawa river with Lake Ontario, bypassing the bottleneck of the St. Lawrence.

Come spring, of course, the canal's ice disappears. The skaters give way to canoes and pleasure craft, for the Rideau canal is one of North America's most scenic water routes. Vacationers hire cruise launches that take them to Kingston on Lake Ontario, 47 locks and 197 km away.

NATIONAL CAPITAL

In 1857 Queen Victoria chose Ottawa as capital of the Province of Canada, and ten years later the Fathers of Confederation adopted it as capital of the Dominion. They were content to leave it within the jurisdiction of the new province of Ontario, but some modern critics believe they made a serious mistake.

Elsewhere, national federations like Canada's have reserved special enclaves for their capitals. The United States has Washington in the District of Columbia. Australia has Canberra in the Australian Capital Territory. In such cases the national capital can remain aloof from regional politics and free from suspicions of prejudice.

In Ottawa's case, however, Ontario's influence is immense. The national capital is the province's third largest city, an important distribution centre and a pillar of its tourism industry. Ontario funds the capital's education system, regulates its hospitals, administers its courts, licences its vehicles, and taxes its inhabitants.

On occasions the influence has been more sinister. One case concerned Louis Riel, who in 1873 and 1874 won election to parliament for a riding in Manitoba. At the time Riel was wanted in Ontario for the 'murder' of Thomas Scott in 1869. As a result he was intimidated from taking his seat in the House of Commons, in case he was arrested.

Provinces elsewhere in Canada have sometimes criticized the national government for being partisan towards Ontario and Quebec, and Quebec has sometimes complained of favour shown towards Ontario. All these factors have persuaded the national government to decentralize its activities, and to spread the benefits of its patronage.

To date, the most significant step in diluting the capital's connections with Ontario was taken in 1969. At a first ministers' conference to discuss constitutional change, it was decided to recognize a 'national capital region,' including not only Ottawa but Hull across the Ottawa river in Quebec and a large area of countryside surrounding them.

Deliberately, many federal departments have been relocated in Hull.

Large office complexes have been built there, and public servants living in Ottawa commute across the river to work. Conversely, many French-speakers from Hull work in Ottawa, helping to emphasize the bilingual status of the national government.

Ottawa and Hull have large permanent populations of several generations standing. They have been joined by Canadians from all parts of the country, most of them associated with government departments or the federal Crown corporations that have headquarters in the capital. Some are there to represent their home regions in parliament.

In addition, of course, Ottawa is the home of missions and legations from countries the world over. Most maintain embassies in Ottawa, but Commonwealth nations contribute high commissions. Their representatives help to give the capital an international flavour quite different from Toronto's and Montreal's.

Ottawa is filled with institutions that buttress the special atmosphere. At the centre of everything is Parliament Hill, its elegant buildings grouped around the famous Peace Tower. The buildings provide fine views of the Ottawa river, and Parliament Hill is sprinkled with statues and monuments.

Not far away is Confederation Square, Ottawa's crossroads, which is dominated by the National War Memorial unveiled in 1939. Overlooking the

Each year, runners from all over central Canada and farther afield converge on Ottawa to take part in the National Capital Marathon.

square are the old Ottawa railroad station, now used as a conference centre, and the National Arts Centre, which was opened in 1969.

The arts centre is one of Ottawa's special prides, built on a hexagonal site beside the Rideau canal. The centre contains an opera house, theatre, and studio theatre, and it features performances by its resident orchestra, two theatre companies (one English, one French), and visiting companies from across Canada.

Many of Canada's national treasures are in Ottawa. The National Gallery holds more than 20 000 paintings, drawings, and prints, a large proportion of them Canadian. The National Library shares its quarters with the Public Archives of Canada, and the National Museum of Natural Sciences is paired with the National Museum of Man.

The Canadian War Museum, the National Museum of Science and Technology, the Post Office Museum, the Supreme Court of Canada, the Royal Canadian Mint — Ottawa is filled with fascination. Not far away is the open country of the Ottawa valley, and in particular Gatineau park, which is the capital's favourite playground.

THE CONSTITUTION

Constitutions are 'systems of fundamental principles that prescribe the nature and functions of states and other institutions.' Some nations have written constitutions, among them the United States. Others, like Britain, rely on unwritten principles hallowed by tradition.

Canada's constitution is partly written, partly unwritten. Many of its principles are enshrined in the British North America Act, passed in 1867 and subsequently much amended. Other principles have been derived from British precedents, Canadian legislation, decisions of the courts, and federal-provincial agreements.

As first enacted, the BNA Act contained 147 clauses that brought the Canadian federation into being and outlined its machinery of government. It created the four original provinces and made allowance for new ones, gave them the right to their own legislatures, and defined their jurisdictions.

For Canada as a whole, the act confirmed the nation's right to govern itself. Only gradually was Canada given the right to control its external affairs, finally confirmed by the Statute of Westminster in 1931. Since then

Canada has been a fully sovereign state, except that parts of its constitution can be amended only if the British parliament co-operates.

Sections of the BNA Act define the various elements of the central government. They include the executive, invested with all the powers of government; parliament, where the voice of the people is expressed; and the judiciary, responsible for the interpretation of laws and the pursuit of justice.

Executive power, according to the act, is vested in the Crown as represented by the governor-general. On a literal interpretation the power appears to be absolute. In practice, it is exercised only on the advice of the governor-general's Privy Council as represented by the cabinet, 'according to the well-understood principles of the British constitution.'

Parliament consists of the Crown, an 'upper house' or Senate, and an elected 'lower house' or House of Commons. Parliament is empowered to pass laws, and as a safeguard, members of the cabinet must answer to parliament for the administration.

The judiciary is by law independent of the other branches of government. Judges are appointed by the Crown on

A bird's eye view of Parliament Hill. Close to the river is the centre block of the parliament buildings, dominated by the Peace Tower. The circular structure behind is the Library of Parliament, which survived the fire of 1916 that destroyed the rest of the block.

the advice of the Privy Council (in fact, the cabinet), but once in office they cannot be removed except in cases of gross misconduct or until they reach retirement age.

Besides defining the elements of Canada's government, the BNA act sets out its areas of jurisdiction, those reserved for the provinces, and a few that are shared. Here, Canada's constitution departs from Britain's and is much closer to that of the United States. Even so, there are major differences that make Canada's unique.

In the United States, those who devised that country's constitution defined the powers of the central government and left the residue to individual states. In Canada the reverse happened. The Fathers of Confederation decided on the powers to be exercised by provinces, and entrusted the residue to the central government.

In general, the powers reserved for the provinces are the ones that affect

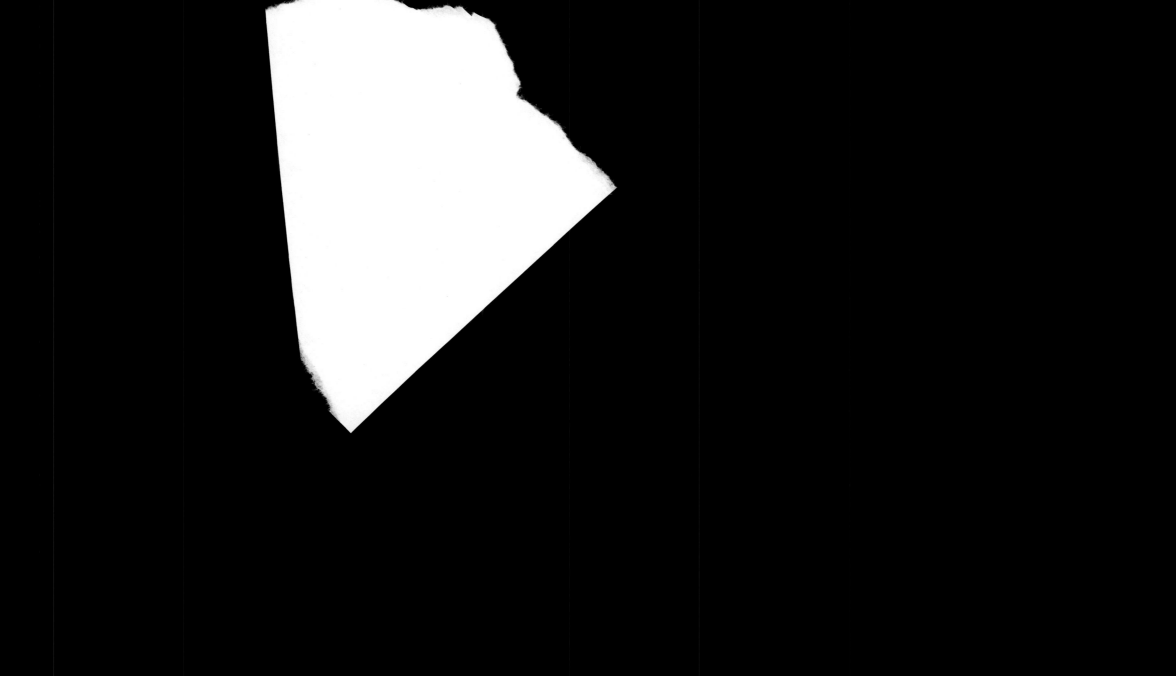

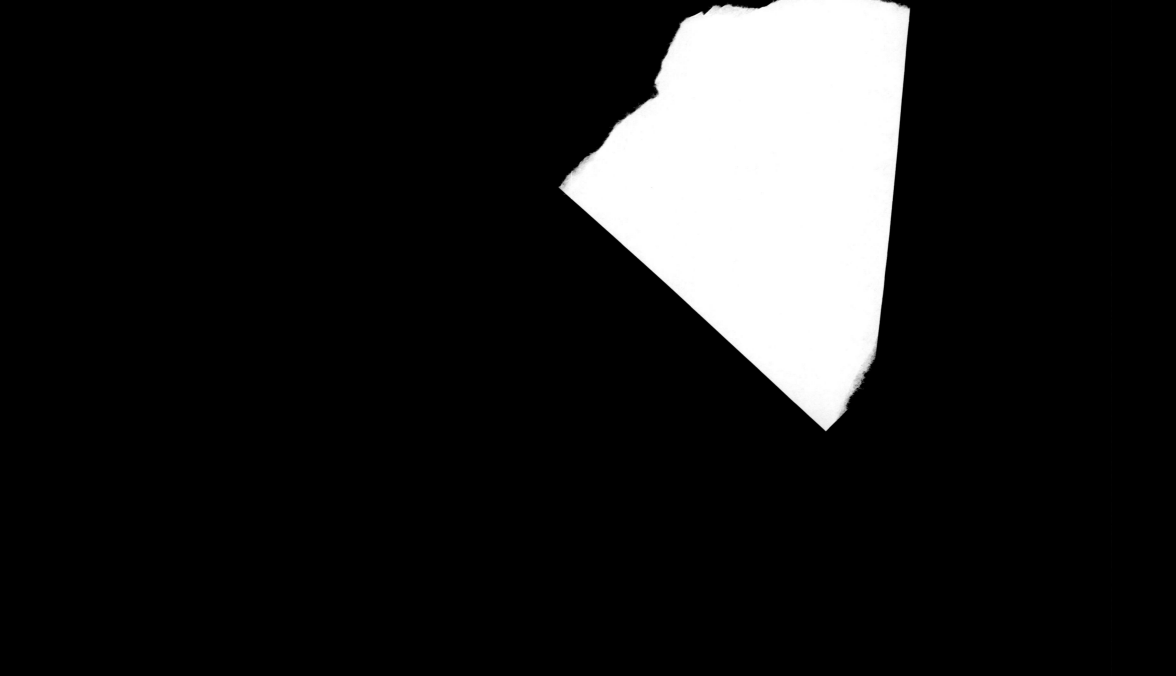

regional concerns. They include control of natural resources, direct taxation for provincial purposes, prisons, hospitals, asylums and charities, municipal institutions, and licenses for provincial and municipal revenue.

Other exclusive powers of the provinces concern local works and undertakings, incorporation of provincial companies, solemnization of marriage, property and civil rights, the administration of justice, matters of a purely local or private nature, and education.

Under the BNA act, parliament and the provinces share responsibility for agriculture and immigration, with the national law prevailing over provincial laws in case of conflicts. Subsequent amendments gave the two levels of government concurrent jurisdictions over pensions, this time with provincial law prevailing.

All other powers were to be vested in the federal government, which was to 'make laws for the peace, order, and good government of Canada in relation to all matters . . . not . . . assigned exclusively to the legislature of the provinces.' The act provided many examples of what this might include.

The examples included defence, raising money by any kind of taxation, regulation of trade and commerce, navigation and shipping, fisheries, money and banking, bankruptcy and insolvency, patents and copyrights, divorce, criminal law and criminal procedure, and penitentiaries.

The act cites several other examples, and subsequent amendments and judicial decisions have highlighted others. Among the federal government's most important responsibilities are interprovincial and international transport and communications, and the aboriginal rights of Inuit and Indians.

One noteworthy omission from the BNA act is any guarantee of fundamental freedoms — for instance, of worship, assembly, and the press. Canadian tradition and the Canadian Bill of Rights passed in 1960 go some way towards filling the gap, but many Canadians would like to see such rights enshrined in the constitution.

Militia regiments change the guard on Parliament Hill. The colourful ceremony is one of Ottawa's treats for tourists.

Official Languages

Under the British North America Act, the houses of parliament may debate in both English and French. The records of both houses must be kept in both languages, acts of parliament must be published in both, and either language may be used in courts set up by parliament.

Those are the constitutional requirements, but parliament and some provinces have gone much further in establishing English and French as the joint official languages of Canada. In 1969 parliament passed the Official Languages Act, giving them equal status for all purposes of Canada's parliament and government.

New Brunswick has made itself officially bilingual, and Ontario has introduced French-language courts and other services in areas with a significant French-speaking population. Many provinces emphasize French as a subject in their educational systems, though Quebec has downplayed English education with the aim of bolstering Québécois culture.

Kings and Queens

In 1497 John Cabot claimed 'Newfoundland' (the coast of North America) for Henry VII of England. In 1534 Jacques Cartier took possession of New France for his sovereign, François I. In 1577 Martin Frobisher annexed Baffin Island for his queen, Elizabeth.

Early explorers were quick to lay claim to their discoveries, and sometimes they overlapped. Even so, the claims established the links that even today commit Canada to ancestral ties with Europe. Apart from brief republican interregna in Newfoundland and Nova Scotia, Canada has always been ruled by royalty.

France's authority in Canada terminated abruptly in 1763, but New France immediately became subject to

On a visit to Rideau Hall in Ottawa, Elizabeth II unveils a plaque commemorating the work of four Canadian-born governors-general.

the sovereigns of Britain. Canada's sovereigns since Confederation have been as follows:

Victoria	1837–1901
Edward VII*	1901–1910
George V*	1910–1936
Edward VIII*	1936
George VI**	1936–1952
Elizabeth II**	1952–

* Visited Canada prior to ascending the throne.
** Visited Canada while sovereign.

On a royal tour of Canada in 1939, George VI and his queen sit in the Canadian Senate to give royal assent to bills passed by parliament.
National Photography Collection C-33278

SOVEREIGN STATE

Since its beginnings as a nation, Canada has been ruled by successive heads of state known as 'the sovereign.' In theory the sovereign's power is absolute. In practice it is exercised only on the recommendation of Canadian advisers who have been sworn in as members of the Privy Council.

The official title of the sovereign is king or queen 'of Canada,' though in practice the monarch also serves as sovereign of Britain, Australia, New Zealand, and several other countries that were part of the British Empire. To date, no sovereign of Canada has resided in the country.

On occasions the sovereign visits Canada, and may then take part in the formal and ceremonial functions carried out in the name of the Crown. These include the summoning, opening, and dissolution of parliament, and assenting to bills previously passed by the House of Commons and Senate.

In normal practice, the role of head of state is delegated to Canada's governor-general, appointed by the sovereign as his or her representative for a term of from five to seven years. The appointment is made on the advice of the Canadian government, and is supposed to be non-partisan.

The governor-general's most important responsibility is to ensure that Canada always has a government. If the prime minister dies or resigns, the governor-general must call on a replacement who can form an administration. According to an Australian precedent, he also has the power to remove a prime minister from office.

No bill can become law without the signature of the governor-general or his deputy, acting for the Crown. He also signs cabinet orders, commissions, pardons, and much else besides. New cabinet ministers are sworn in before the governor-general or his deputy. The governor-general acts as commander-in-chief of Canada's armed forces.

Foreign ambassadors present their letters of credence to the governor-general on arriving in Ottawa, and he receives high commissioners from the Commonwealth too. He is head and principal companion of the Order of Canada and conducts investitures into

Rideau Hall is the governor-general's official home in Ottawa. For part of the year he may reside in the Citadel in Quebec City.

that order and others. He also awards decorations for bravery.

As an acting head of state, the governor-general is entitled to be kept informed on important government matters. Depending on his relationship with the prime minister, he may be consulted on appropriate courses of action. In any case, he has the right to caution the prime minister, though his advice may not be heeded.

The governor-general has two official residences during his term in office, Rideau Hall in Ottawa and the Citadel in Quebec City. By tradition he spends much of his time travelling across Canada to meet the Canadians he is serving, and on occasion represents Canada abroad by paying official visits to other countries.

The Governors-General

Until 1926, Canada's governors-general doubled as representatives of the monarch and agents of the British government. Then the second responsibility was eliminated and appointments were made subject to Canada's approval. Since 1952, governors-general have been of Canadian birth, appointed by the sovereign but recommended by the Canadian government.

Governors-general since Confederation have been as follows:

Viscount Monck	1867–1868
Lord Lisgar	1868–1872
Earl of Dufferin	1872–1878
Marquess of Lorne	1878–1883
Marquess of Lansdowne	1883–1888
Lord Stanley	1888–1893
Earl of Aberdeen	1893–1898
Earl of Minto	1898–1904
Earl Grey	1904–1911
Duke of Connaught	1911–1916
Duke of Devonshire	1916–1921
Lord Byng of Vimy	1921–1926
Viscount Willingdon	1926–1931

Earl of Bessborough	1931–1935
Lord Tweedsmuir	1935–1940
Earl of Athlone	1940–1946
Viscount Alexander	1946–1952
Vincent Massey	1952–1959
Georges-P. Vanier	1959–1967
Roland Michener	1967–1974

Jules Léger	1974–1979
Edward Schreyer	1979–

A rare photograph of three Canadian governors-general and their ladies, together at Rideau Hall. From left are Jules and Gaby Léger, Edward and Lily Schreyer, and Roland and Norah Michener.

Prime Ministers

The prime minister is the parliamentary leader requested by the governor-general to form an administration. By custom he is the leader best able to command majority support in the House of Commons. He is expected to choose the cabinet of ministers that serves as the committee of the Privy Council.

By custom, the prime minister remains in office as long as he retains the confidence of the House of Commons. If a motion of 'no confidence' is introduced and he is defeated, he must immediately resign and with him his whole administration. Similarly, he is expected to resign if his party is defeated in a general election.

Among the prime minister's special powers is the right to recommend that the governor-general dissolve parliament and call an election. He has complete control of the organization of the cabinet and can shuffle ministers as he wishes. Many of the governor-general's appointees are chosen on his recommendation, among them the provincial lieutenant-governors and all senators.

The prime minister's informal responsibilities include representing Canada in meetings with the first ministers of other lands, negotiating with the premiers of the provinces at federal-provincial conferences, and acting as spokesman for his administration before the House of Commons.

To date, most of Canada's administrations have been drawn from the two major parties, the Liberals (L) and Conservatives (C) or Progressive Conservatives (PC), as the Conservatives have been since uniting with the Progressive Party in 1942. During World War I a Union (U) administration included elements of both sides. Here is a list of Canada's prime ministers:

Sir John A. Macdonald (C)	1867–1873
Alexander Mackenzie (L)	1873–1878
Sir John A. Macdonald (C)	1878–1891
Sir John Abbott (C)	1891–1892
Sir John Thompson (C)	1892–1894
Sir Mackenzie Bowell (C)	1894–1896
Sir Charles Tupper (C)	1896
Sir Wilfrid Laurier (L)	1896–1911
Sir Robert Borden (C)	1911–1917
Sir Robert Borden (U)	1917–1920
Arthur Meighen (U)	1920–1921
Mackenzie King (L)	1921–1926
Arthur Meighen (C)	1926
Mackenzie King (L)	1926–1930
R. B. Bennett (C)	1930–1935
Mackenzie King (L)	1935–1948
Louis St. Laurent (L)	1948–1957
John Diefenbaker (PC)	1957–1963
Lester Pearson (L)	1963–1968
Pierre Trudeau (L)	1968–1979
Joseph Clark (PC)	1979–

Macdonald

Mackenzie

Abbott

Thompson

Bowell

Tupper

Laurier

Borden

Meighen

Mackenzie King

Bennett

St. Laurent

Diefenbaker

Pearson

Trudeau

Clark

THE CABINET

The BNA act provides for a 'Council to aid and advise in the Government of Canada, to be styled the Queen's Privy Council for Canada.' Its distinguished membership includes past governors-general, past and present cabinet ministers and provincial premiers, and past and present speakers of parliament.

By tradition, all executive acts of the federal government are carried out in the name of the monarch in council or the governor-general in council. In fact, the Privy Council as a whole is never consulted. Its 'aid and advice' is provided through a committee of the Privy Council informally known as the cabinet.

Members of the committee or cabinet are chosen by the prime minister, himself appointed by the governor-general. Both the prime minister and ministers of his cabinet must be sworn to the Privy Council before they may enter office. Once admitted, they remain members for life, even after political defeat.

One other stipulation affects membership of the cabinet. Under the rules of responsible government, ministers are accountable to parliament. If they are not already members of the Senate or House of Commons, then seats must be found for them, whether through ap-

pointment (to the Senate) or by-elections (to the House of Commons).

Traditionally, Canada's cabinets include at least one representative of each province, and where possible, of each region of the country. It is a way of ensuring that local interests are not forgotten. Otherwise the ministers chosen are picked for their abilities and their special knowledge and experience.

Some ministers may join the cabinet 'without portfolio,' but most are given responsibility for one or more departments of the administration and probably for various Crown agencies too. There are also 'ministers of state' appointed to assist senior ministers or to develop new policies in areas of government not adequately covered.

The cabinet regularly meets in full to

Following its election in 1979, Joseph Clark's cabinet poses for photographs with Edward Schreyer, Canada's governor-general.

discuss its policies and decide on action. However, much of the ministers' work is done in small cabinet committees that ensure thorough study of the proposals. The organization and composition of cabinet committees is decided by the prime minister.

Discussion that takes place in these committees and in meetings of the full cabinet is confidential. All ministers take an oath of secrecy, and once a decision is made, they are expected to support it. If they want to express disagreement in public, they are required to resign rather than break the rule of cabinet solidarity.

Ministers speak for their departments in the cabinet, in parliament, and in public. Here, external affairs minister Flora Mac-Donald talks to the media.

PARLIAMENT

Like Britain's Westminster, Canada's parliament has three components. One is the Crown as represented by the governor-general. The second is the 'upper house,' in Canada known as the Senate. The third is the House of Commons.

Of the three, the most important in a modern parliamentary democracy is the House of Commons. No Canadian government can hold office without the Commons' consent, and government ministers are answerable to the Commons for the activities and failures of departments of the government.

Most government ministers are themselves members of the Commons, and like the others they represent the interests of individual constituencies.

The boundaries of constituencies are reviewed following each decennial census, and may be redrawn in time for the next general election.

For the election held in 1979, Canada was divided into 282 constituencies. Newfoundland had 7, Prince Edward Island 4, Nova Scotia 11, New Brunswick 10, Quebec 75, Ontario 95, Manitoba 14, Saskatchewan 14, Alberta 21, British Columbia 28, the Yukon 1, and the Northwest Territories 2.

Election is the only route to membership of the Commons. Members of the Senate, however, are appointed by the governor-general on the recommendation of the prime minister. Senators must be at least 30 years of age, must be 'subjects of the sovereign,' and must fulfil certain property and residential requirements.

From the beginning, the Senate has been organized to represent Canada's regions. Under the BNA act, each of four regions (Ontario, Quebec, the Maritimes, and the western provinces) has the right to 24 seats in the Senate. Newfoundland has the right to six, and the Yukon and Northwest Territories to one apiece.

In addition, the BNA act makes it possible for the governor-general to appoint additional senators for the four regions. The provision is helpful when a government faces a hostile majority in the upper house, or when the prime minister wants to recruit new regional representatives to his cabinet.

Adorned by a maple leaf, the Peace Tower on Parliament Hill is the centrepiece of a dramatic Canada Day fireworks display.

John A. Macdonald suggested that one of the chief purposes of the Senate was to provide 'sober second thought' on the deliberations of the Commons. Accordingly, most of Canada's senators are appointed in recognition of previous public service, and the majority stay in office until obliged to retire at 75.

Much of the Senate's work is done in special investigative and legislative committees that probe aspects of the national life seldom neglected by the Commons. The committees' recommendations are often embodied in legislation introduced in the Senate and later transmitted to the Commons for debate.

Both the Senate and the Commons are housed in the parliament buildings, but they are separate organizations. They have separate chambers and administrations, and they are served by separate Speakers who preside over their debates and act as their spokesmen to the Crown and to the public.

The Commons' Speaker is elected by his fellow members at the beginning of a parliamentary session. In practice, he has been selected by the prime minister. The Senate's Speaker is appointed by the governor-general, once more on the prime minister's advice.

Parliament must meet at least once a year, and there are two occasions when its three components come together. One is the opening of parliament, the other the closing. By Westminster tradition, the sovereign may not enter the Commons, so the ceremonies always take place in the Senate.

For the opening the Speaker's chair serves as a throne for the sovereign if he or she is present, or otherwise for the governor-general. Senators occupy their usual places and the Commons crowd into the aisle. Then the sovereign or governor-general reads the 'speech from the throne.'

The speech deals in general terms with the state of the country and outlines the legislation that the government plans for the session. Though delivered in the name of the Crown, the speech has been prepared by the prime minister and the cabinet who are wholly responsible for what it contains.

General Elections

Under the constitution there must be a general election for the Commons at least once every five years. With few exceptions, every Canadian citizen over the age of 18 has the right to vote. Again with few exceptions, anyone eligible to vote can be nominated as a candidate.

When an election has been called, complicated machinery is set in motion. Across the country, returning officers responsible for individual constituencies appoint enumerators to compile lists of voters, arrange polling divisions and polling stations, and prepare to count the votes cast.

There is no need for a candidate to reside in the constituency he or she is contesting. However, the nomination must be endorsed by at least 25 eligible voters of the constituency, and must name an official agent and auditor who will be present when the votes are counted.

To deter frivolous nominations, candidates must put up a deposit of $200. Deposits are returned to candidates who win election or who poll more than 15 per cent of the total votes cast. Otherwise they are forfeited. In most cases nominations close 21 days before the election.

Some candidates stand as independents, but most are nominated by political parties. The largest parties in Canada operate at three levels — national, provincial, and constituency. The various constituency associations choose their own candidates for elections and send delegates to party conventions to vote on party policies.

Since Confederation, the dominant forces in Canadian politics have been the Liberal Party and the Conservative or (since 1942) Progressive Conservative Party. Two smaller parties regularly represented in parliament are the New Democratic Party and Social Credit.

MAKING LAWS

A parliament's fundamental role is to serve as a talking place where grievances can be aired and public policies debated. Beyond that, most parliaments have supervisory control over the executive branch of government. Their most prominent function, however, is quite separate — the power to make laws.

In Canada, parliament's procedures in enacting laws are broadly similar to

those evolved at Westminster. With one major exception, proposed laws (bills) may be introduced in either of the houses of parliament. Before they become law, however, they must be passed by both Senate and Commons and must receive the assent of the Crown.

The exception concerns 'money bills,' those involving appropriation of public funds or imposing taxation. Appropriation bills stem from the government's estimates of what funds it re-

The House of Commons, the key element in Canada's parliamentary democracy.

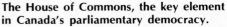

quires, based on departmental reviews, and taxation bills are based on proposals in the budget. Such bills have to be introduced in the Commons by a minister of the government.

Some bills are private, affecting a particular institution or group of people, and they are usually introduced in the Senate. The great majority, however, are public. Most have been prepared by a department of the administration in consultation with other departments, and are sponsored by the minister responsible.

A bill introduced to the Commons is initially given 'first reading.' There is no debate at this stage, but with the motion for first reading carried, the bill is automatically ordered for reading 'at the next sitting.' Meanwhile, copies of the bill are distributed so that members can see what it entails.

On a later occasion, the member sponsoring the bill moves that it be read a second time. On this motion, members debate the principle of the bill but not its specific provisions. With the motion carried, the bill is considered to be approved in principle and is referred to a standing committee for detailed study.

The Commons (and the Senate also) tends to rely heavily on standing committees to relieve its heavy workload. Each committee includes up to 30 members drawn from both the government party and the opposition, and is entrusted with the task of summoning expert witnesses and hearing evidence relating to bills in a specific field of policy.

At the committee stage, amendments may be proposed and adopted. The committee reports the results of its study to the Commons, and further amendments may be proposed. Only rarely are bills considered by the Committee of the Whole, the complete Commons sitting without the Speaker.

As a final step in the Commons, the bill receives a third reading. If it is passed, it is transmitted to the Senate where it follows a similar route. Again there are four main stages — first reading, second reading, detailed study, and final reading.

The Senate may propose amendments to bills from the Commons, and vice versa. If the other house concurs in the amendments, the bill goes forward for royal assent. If not, there may be a 'free conference' at which representatives of both houses meet to discuss and resolve their differences.

The Senate has an absolute right to vote on all bills, and so has the Commons. Both houses have the right to amend legislation, but with money bills the Senate may only reduce the proposed appropriation or reduce the tax imposed. In practice, the system has produced few deadlocks.

When both houses have passed the bill and concurred with any amendments, it goes forward for royal assent. The monarch, the governor-general, or his deputy sign the bill and make it an act of parliament. Some acts come into force on the day of signature; some are reserved to be proclaimed at a later date.

The parliament buildings are Ottawa's leading tourist attraction. Most visitors are admitted through the central lobby that leads to the Senate, House of Commons, and Library of Parliament.

Money Matters

On the first day of a session, the House of Commons normally passes two government motions without comment. One sets up a Committee of Ways and Means, the other a Commitee of Supply.

In practice the two committees consist of all members of the Commons sitting under a chairman instead of the Speaker. The Committee of Ways and Means considers taxation policies; the Committee of Supply considers how taxation revenue should be spent once it has been collected.

Early in the session, the government minister of finance introduces an 'interim supply bill' designed to provide the government with enough money to meet its commitments until its full estimates have been approved. Meanwhile, each department of the government prepares estimates of what it will need in the coming financial year.

The various estimates are revised and co-ordinated by the government's Treasury Board, and are then presented to the house as a 'blue book.' In due course they are considered in the Committee of Supply. Once approved, they are included in an appropriation bill or bills introduced by the minister of finance.

The minister explains the appropriations in his budget speech, one of the great occasions of the parliamentary year. The speech traditionally accompanies the second reading of the chief appropriation bill. In it he estimates the revenue that may be expected from existing taxation, and if necessary may propose new or revised taxes to produce more.

One by one the taxation proposals are considered by the Committee of Ways and Means. When adopted they are incorporated in a money bill that must follow the usual route before it can become law. In this way the Commons asserts its right to protect the taxpayer and supervise the management of the public purse.

THE COURTS

Parliament and the provincial legislatures pass laws, and the federal and provincial administrations put them into effect. When disputes arise, the law can be interpreted by the judiciary. This amounts to a third arm of government quite separate from the other two.

The judiciary includes all Canada's judges — some federal, some provincial, some territorial. Senior judges are known as 'justices,' appointed by the federal government to serve in its own courts and in senior courts created by the provinces. The others are 'judges,' appointed by the provinces and territories to serve in their lesser courts.

The highest court in the land is the Supreme Court of Canada, located in Ottawa and established in 1875. The court consists of nine justices, of whom at least three must be from Quebec, reflecting the special character of Quebec's civil law. By custom, three are from Ontario, one from Atlantic Canada, and two from the western provinces.

One important function of the Supreme Court is to give advisory opinions to the federal government as requested.

Otherwise its work is to hear appeals. Some appeals concern criminal cases, some civil, and all but a few stem from decisions of the various provincial and territorial courts of appeal.

In criminal cases, the Supreme Court will hear an appeal in respect of serious offences where an acquittal has been set aside or where a judge of a provincial court of appeal had dissented on a point of law. Besides, the court will hear appeals on any point of law, providing it is of sufficient public importance.

Civil appellants have the right to be heard in the Supreme Court if the relevant provincial court of appeal has given permission. Otherwise, the Supreme Court may itself give leave to appeal if it is satisfied that the case is of sufficient public importance or if there is an important issue of law or fact or both.

Twice a month during their three sessions each year, the justices of the Supreme Court sit on panels of three to hear motions for leave to appeal. Cases they accept are heard by the court as a whole, consisting of five, seven, or all nine justices as suits the occasion.

The Supreme Court of Canada is administered by the federal Department

The Supreme Court of Canada consists of nine justices of appeal. At least three of them must be from Quebec.

of Justice, and so is its cousin, the Federal Court. Originally created as the Exchequer Court in 1875, the Federal Court considers matters of federal jurisdiction, including taxation and claims involving the federal government. It was reconstituted in 1970 and has both trial and appeal divisions.

Under the British North America Act, the provinces (and by extension the territories) have extensive powers in the administration of justice. These powers include setting up and maintaining courts of civil and criminal jurisdiction, and in setting out the procedures that will be used in civil matters in those courts.

Most provinces favour a three-tiered court system consisting of a high court, intermediate level, and various lesser courts. Names vary from province to province, but the structure is much the same. In each case, a rigid distinction is drawn between the courts' civil and criminal jurisdictions.

Typically, the high court of the pro-

Even though it shares Parliament Hill with the parliament buildings, the Supreme Court of Canada is the symbol of an independent judiciary.

vince or territory is divided into trial and appeal divisions. Quebec's is known as the Superior Court, Saskatchewan's and Alberta's as Courts of Queen's Bench, and the remainder as Supreme Courts. Intermediate courts are usually known as county or district courts, and lesser courts are provincial or territorial.

Civil law is used to settle private disputes between individuals and other private parties. Most civil suits involve sums of money, and the amounts help to determine which level of court hears them. The majority go to a 'small claims court' or its equivalent, a wing of the provincial or territorial courts.

Each province makes its own civil law, but Canada's criminal law is created by the federal government and is standard across the country. The criminal code defines crimes, in other words offences regarded as harmful to all or part of the community rather than simply to another individual, and fixes appropriate penalties.

In Toronto, the federal court is housed in the impressive headquarters of an insurance company.

Some criminal cases are reserved for the provincial court, some for the high court. Some can be heard in either the provincial or intermediate court, depending on the wishes of the accused.

All 'summary conviction' cases — those with maximum penalties of $500 fines or six months imprisonment or both — are heard by the provincial and territorial courts.

PUBLIC SERVICE

In theory, the government departments and agencies that make up the federal public service are attached to the executive. In practice, some political scientists count the public service or administration as a fourth arm of government. Cabinets may be swept out of office, but the public service survives no matter what party is in power.

When originally formed, the federal administration consisted of a handful of departments employing a few thousand civil servants. As Canada has grown, so has the public service. New departments and agencies have been created as necessary, and the federal administration employs nearly 300 000 public servants across the country.

Full-fledged departments of the administration fall into two categories. Some are 'line' departments, functioning in a specialized field like agriculture, external affairs, or national defence. Others are 'domestic' departments whose activities span the whole field of government. They include the Treasury

A charming statue in Ottawa lampoons the rush hour as busy civil servants hurry to work. In practice, public servants' work hours are deliberately staggered.

Board and the Department of Finance.

Each department is headed by a minister who speaks for it in the cabinet, in parliament, and in public. Advising him is his deputy minister, the department's senior public servant. The deputy minister and his assistants are expected to apply the law as made by parliament and to carry out the instructions of the cabinet as passed on by the minister.

Take, for example, the Department of Consumer and Corporate Affairs. The department administers more than 20 acts of parliament, from the Bankruptcy Act to the Weights and Measures Act. It is divided into four branches, each responsible for different fields of policy and for innovating new programs as necessary.

Another example is the Department of National Revenue, which functions in two components. National Revenue, Customs and Excise, assesses and collects duties and sales and excise taxes. National Revenue, Taxation, assesses and collects income taxes and payments under the Canada Pension Plan and Unemployment Insurance Act.

In the lunch hour, public servants mingle with tourists at a terrace restaurant beside the Rideau Canal.

The Mandarins

When the federal bureaucracy was smaller, it was headed by an élite group of senior public servants known as 'the mandarins.' Members of the group tended to be English-speaking and Protestant, they had been educated at the same universities, and they regularly conferred with each other at the exclusive Rideau Club.

It was sometimes claimed that mandarins had more authority than the ministers they were serving. Certainly many of them had far more knowledge and experience, and their informal meetings were said to accomplish as much as meetings of the cabinet. They were counted among the most powerful men in Canada.

Some of the mandarins survive, but their exclusive fraternity has been dispersed. Departments are much larger than they used to be, and deputy ministers have been joined by assistant deputies who themselves command legions of public servants and control budgets amounting to millions of dollars.

During the 1970s the old dominance of English-speakers and Protestants steadily declined. Many more senior public servants are French-speaking or from minority groups. Perhaps the bitterest blow to the mandarin tradition, the Rideau Club is no

Ottawa's Rideau Club is famous as the meeting-place of mandarins, the senior public servants who used to dominate the federal bureaucracy.

longer the only place in Ottawa that serves a fine meal in pleasant surroundings.

By the late 1970s the federal public service included some 25 separate departments, most of them with offices in all regions of Canada. In addition, there were many times that number of specialized public agencies for which individual ministers were accountable to parliament, just as they were for their departments.

The legal status of these public agencies varies greatly, but they were described as boards, commissions, or Crown corporations. Their staffs are all public servants, though in many cases they are not under the direct political control of the cabinet but function as independent entities.

Statistics Canada, the St. Lawrence Seaway Authority, the Immigration Appeal Board, the Metric Commission — there are government agencies handling everything from pensions to peniten-

Since 1969 the national capital has consisted not only of Ottawa but also of Hull across the Ottawa river in Quebec. Many federal departments have been relocated in Hull and public servants commute there to work.

tiaries and from farm credit to freshwater fish. Among the agencies are the National Energy Board, Air Canada, and the Medical Research Council.

Two of the administrative bodies are unlike all the others. One is the Privy

Council office, which is really the cabinet secretariat. The other is the federal-provincial relations office, an offshoot of the Privy Council office that liaises with provincial governments across the country.

THE GUARDIANS

Together with beavers and maple leaves, the stetsons and scarlet jackets of the Mounties are recognized everywhere as symbols of Canada. Children all over the world grow up believing that 'the Mountie always gets his man,' and no other national police force surpasses the RCMP's deep-rooted reputation for bravery and integrity.

The Royal Canadian (then North West) Mounted Police was formed in 1873 to bring law and order to Western Canada and prevent the United States from occupying it. Threats from the United States took the force to the Yukon in the 1890s, in time to police the Klondike gold rush and make it the most peaceful on record.

The Mounties proved their worth so frequently that the government of Canada steadily increased their responsibilities. From the beginning they were put in charge of customs and excise in Western Canada. After 1896 police officers were expected to serve as immigration officials, land agents, and welfare officers as well.

The force became 'royal' in 1904, by courtesy of Edward VII. In 1920 it absorbed the Dominion Police of Eastern Canada, thus becoming the sole federal police force. In 1928 it was contracted by Saskatchewan to provide police services in the province, and since then has signed similar contracts with all provinces except Ontario and Quebec.

Hollywood has done much to build

an image of Mounties as men of the frontier, tougher than the social outcasts they are policing and a match for the worst weather that nature can throw against them. Today's Mounties spurn the image, but real-life stories of the force show it is not totally undeserved.

There was, for instance, the saga of the Mad Trapper in 1932. The trapper was Albert Johnson of the Mackenzie delta, who had been tampering with Indian traplines. In separate incidents the Mad Trapper wounded one Mountie and killed a second, and escaped to the Yukon before a patrol finally ran him to ground. He was killed in the final shoot-out.

A happier story concerns the RCMP vessel *St. Roch*, a wooden motor schooner that between 1940 and 1942 sailed from Vancouver to Halifax by way of the northwest passage. In 1944 the schooner sailed back to Vancouver by the same route, and went on to become the first vessel to circumnavigate North America.

The Mounties, then, have come to wear many hats. Mountie contingents have several times gone to war. Today's Mounties patrol highways in eight provinces, they man customs cutters on watch for smugglers, they research crimes, they protect migratory birds, and they administer immigration and passport control.

The force's headquarters is in Ottawa, with a commissioner in charge who is responsible to Canada's solicitor-general. The commissioner is assisted by three deputy commissioners, who head criminal operations, administration, and pooled police services, and by the director-general of the RCMP's security service.

The security service is little understood by those outside it, even by other members of the force. Its duty is to protect Canada's internal security, so its

Customs and excise rank high among the RCMP's responsibilities. Here, a high-powered launch and helicopter patrol the coast of Newfoundland.

officers collect information about organizations that could be dangerous. The officers usually act in strict secrecy, and only rarely does news of security activities reach the public.

Outside Ottawa, the RCMP is organized in divisions that police individual provinces and territories. Ontario and Quebec have their own provincial police forces and most of Canada's cities and large towns have municipal forces, but the other provinces, territories, and municipalities contract the RCMP.

The Mounties aside, there are several other protective agencies employed by the federal government. One is the Canadian Coast Guard, an arm of the department of transport that makes Canada's sea lanes safe and protects the marine environment. The Coast Guard operates buoys, lighthouses, weather ships, and a fleet of icebreakers.

The Coast Guard co-operates with Maritime Command of the Defence Force in launching search and rescue operations for vessels in trouble. Coast Guard vessels and aircraft of the Defence Force's Air Command patrol Canada's 200-nautical-mile fisheries zone, and Transport Canada's air traffic controllers regulate the skies.

In all provinces except Ontario and Quebec, the RCMP is contracted to provide provincial police services.

Penitentiaries

Canada has three types of correctional institution. One is the training school for juvenile offenders, operated by a provincial government or a private organization. The second is the provincial institute for adults. The third is the federal penitentiary for adults serving sentences of over two years.

There are now some 50 federal penitentiaries across Canada, among them Kingston penitentiary in Ontario which was opened in 1835. Penitentiaries are graded as maximum, medium, and minimum security institutions, allowing progressively greater privileges to their inmates depending on their good behaviour.

On sentencing by a court, inmates first attend a reception centre run by the Canadian Penitentiary Service.

There they are tested to decide what degree of security they need, and what form of training they might be suited for. A key element of the penitentiary system is equipping inmates to lead useful lives.

Maximum security institutions, like Kingston or New Brunswick's Dorchester, enforce strict security arrangements with armed towers around the perimeter. Medium security institutions can be less strict, but still have armed towers. Minimum security institutions are not enclosed.

Depending on circumstances, inmates may be granted temporary absence from the institution, with or without escort. They may also earn parole, a form of conditional release before the end of their sentence. Often inmates approaching full parole are granted day parole to help them gradually readjust to life outside.

EXTERNAL AFFAIRS

When Pierre Trudeau campaigned for election in 1968, he made only one election promise. That was to review Canada's foreign policy. In particular, he wanted to reassess Canada's role in the North Atlantic Treaty Organisation, and to negotiate diplomatic relations with the People's Republic of China.

The promise suggested a radical break with Canada's traditional external policy, best analyzed as 'U.S. plus U.K. divided by two.' Long buttressed by its special relationships with Britain and the United States, Canada tended to view the world from their points of view and take action accordingly.

Now Trudeau was considering alternatives. After prolonged negotiations, Canada decided to remain within

The Lester Pearson building in Ottawa is the headquarters of Canada's Department of External Affairs.

The Commonwealth

Canada enjoys special relationships with the United States and *La Francophonie*, the French-speaking world. It plays a full part in the affairs of the United Nations and its agencies. On a less formal level it belongs to the association known as the Commonwealth of Nations.

The Commonwealth, of course, is descended from the British Empire. It includes Britain and the independent countries once governed by Britain that choose to be members. In the late 1970s some 35 countries belonged, amounting to roughly one-quarter of the world's nations and representing a large part of its population.

Some of the countries are monarchies, some republics, but all recognize Queen Elizabeth as head of the Commonwealth. Every two years their heads of government meet to exchange ideas on their countries' affairs and the state of the world. No votes are taken, but the leaders can reach consensus that leads to united action.

At other times, Commonwealth ministers confer on issues such as trade policy or food production. Education, forestry, scientific research, law, medicine, and communications are only some of the common interests regularly discussed. Since 1975, member nations have considered ways of lessening the gap between rich and poor.

In a formal organization, ideological and geographical differences might force the various Commonwealth members to take contradictory stands. In the voluntary association, they rely on their common connection with Britain to forge ties with each other. Basing their relationship on fundamental common sense, they promote international peace and good will far beyond their borders.

The Canadian International Development Agency funds special projects in developing countries. Here, a CIDA instructor leads a metal-turning class at a secondary school on St. Lucia in the Caribbean, a member of the Commonwealth.

NATO but to reduce its troop commitments. Before long, Canada proceeded to recognize China and exchange ambassadors, one of the first western democracies to do so.

These early successes led the Trudeau administration to define a new foreign policy for Canada. The objective was to deploy Canadian skills and resources wherever they might do the most good, not merely where they would be politically expedient or help to promote a particular image.

For many years, Canada had been sharing its wealth with less fortunate countries, especially with those of Southern and South-Eastern Asia. Now the policy was extended to nations of Africa and the Caribbean too. Loans and gifts were made available through the Canadian International Development Agency.

Meanwhile, the government was reassessing Canada's relationship with the United States. The two countries were closely involved in joint defence programs and each other's trade and commerce. Improving communications meant they were becoming inseparable in a cultural sense too.

The government decided it had three options. One was to allow the status quo to continue, the second was to press for even closer integration, and the third was to strive for Canadian nationalism. It chose the third option, and consciously set out to develop economic and cultural ties outside North America.

That policy remains a major influence. Canada has cultivated strong trading links with the European Economic Community, Japan, and Latin America. Besides, Canada has reinforced its strong cultural bonds with members of the Commonwealth and of *La Francophonie*, countries of the French-speaking world.

At the United Nations, Canada takes special interest in the developing countries, which comprise about two-thirds of the membership. With its own population drawn from all over the globe, Canada is a microcosm of the United Nations community. Besides, Canada is a prominent contributor to the UN's specialized agencies.

One of the agencies, the International Civil Aviation Organization, has

its headquarters in Montreal. Others include the World Health Organization, Food and Agriculture Organization, United Nations Educational, Scientific and Cultural Organization, International Monetary Fund, and the Universal Postal Union.

Canada maintains a permanent mission at the United Nations, where it is represented by an ambassador and officials of the Department of External Affairs. The department also maintains a permanent mission at the European Economic Community, as well as some 60 embassies and 20 high commissions to countries around the world.

Typically, the embassies and high commissions are staffed not only by diplomats from External Affairs but also by representatives of other departments. Trade attachés represent the Department of Industry, Trade and Commerce; and immigration, cultural, and military attachés have important duties.

Besides representing Canada's politi-

Canada and the United States share the world's longest undefended border, part of it the section between the Yukon and Alaska.

cal interests in the various host countries, the diplomats are expected to collect information about local developments of interest to Canada. The information is collated and interpreted at External Affairs headquarters in Ottawa, and foreign policy recommendations are made to the government.

One factor complicating the work of the diplomats is that the federal government cannot bind the provinces to follow its external policies. Quebec, for one, has pursued a vigorous foreign policy of its own, and several others maintain permanent missions in the United States and Europe.

Foreign diplomats are close to the heart of the national capital's social whirl. This is a garden party in the grounds of Rideau Hall.

Keeping the Peace

In 1956, Egypt seized and nationalized the Suez canal, which belonged to Britain and France. After issuing an ultimatum without result, the two countries attacked, but Russia threatened immediate retaliation against their capitals. The United States demanded that the two countries immediately withdraw their troops.

The crisis rapidly escalated, and there was a real chance of world war. Lester Pearson, then Canada's minister of external affairs, proposed that the United Nations send an emergency force to restore peace in the canal zone. The powers in the conflict could then honourably withdraw from their extreme commitments.

The force was sent, with Canada contributing its commander and the

A Lynx reconnaissance vehicle in Cyprus, part of the Canadian contribution to the United Nations peace-keeping force.

largest number of troops. The Suez crisis was averted, and Lester Pearson was awarded the Nobel peace prize for 1957. Ever since, Canada has taken special pride in its role as a peacekeeper, and has sent troops to many of the world's trouble spots.

In the 1960s Canadian contingents joined UN forces in Cyprus, Israel, the Belgian Congo (Zaire), Nigeria, and Yemen. In the 1970s units were sent to Egypt, Syria, and Lebanon, all serving in the UN's famous blue berets. At the close of the decade, Canada's largest UN commitments were in Cyprus and on the Golan heights between Israel and Syria.

NATIONAL DEFENCE

Canada ended World War II as one of the world's leading military powers. The armed forces were in three separate branches — army, navy, and air force. Each branch had its own bases, equipment, personnel, and chain of command.

With that organization Canada became a founding member of the North Atlantic Treaty Organization (NATO) in 1949. NATO was designed as a defensive alliance linking North America with Western Europe that would counterbalance the military strength of Russia and the nations of the Warsaw Pact.

In a sense, Canada had long been part of an Atlantic triangle. The country had a special relationship with Britain, and close contact with the United States. The balance helped Canada to develop a special military role of its own, helping to keep the peace in world trouble spots on behalf of the United Nations.

In 1957 Canada and the United States formed the North American Air Defence Command (NORAD). This time the objective was to defend the two countries against the threat of attack from Russia. If war broke out between Russia and the United States, it seemed Canada would be the battleground.

To warn the two countries of approaching attack, three lines of radar stations had been built across the continent. One, the Pinetree, stretched from Vancouver to Newfoundland. The Mid-Canada line followed the 55th parallel. The Distant Early Warning (DEW) line ran north of the arctic circle.

The building of the DEW line helped to strengthen Canada's sovereignty over its northern possessions, and control is confirmed by regular air patrols and the construction of northern bases. Canada remains committed to both NATO and NORAD, but since the middle 1960s, the country has steadily reduced its defence resources.

Starting in 1964, the three armed services were integrated as a single force. Then the manpower was pruned. By the late 1970s there were about 80 000 personnel in the permanent force, down from 120 000 in the middle

The helicopter-carrying destroyer HMCS Skeena **on patrol off Canada's east coast.**

1960s. The force is organized in four commands and three headquarters.

The commands and two of the headquarters report to National Defence Headquarters in Ottawa. In control there is the chief of the defence staff, the senior military adviser to the minister of defence, who is responsible for all aspects of the armed forces' administration, operations, and personnel.

The old role of Canada's army is today borne by Mobile Command, which has one brigade group in Western Canada, one in the east, and a paratrooper combat group that includes the highly trained Special Service Force. Mobile Command also contains the Canadian peace-keeping contingents in Cyprus and the Middle East.

Maritime Command wears the mantle of the Royal Canadian Navy, and has its principal bases in Halifax and Esquimalt. Besides manning Canada's warships, the command controls the maritime aircraft that patrol the 200-nautical-mile fisheries zones declared by Canada in 1977.

Air Command has its headquarters in Winnipeg. Its air defence group maintains the sovereignty of Canada's air space, equipped with fighter squadrons

Two Canadian Voodoo fighters attached to NORAD patrol air space over the Rocky mountains.

and control of the Pinetree and DEW radar lines. The Mid-Canada line was given up in the mid-1960s.

Search and rescue operations and airlifts of troops and equipment are responsibilities of Air Command's air transport group. Canadian Forces Communications Command (CFCC) provides strategic communications for the whole defence force, and Canadian Forces Northern Region controls an area extending to the north pole.

The Royal 22nd (Van Doos), Canada's only francophone regiment, parades at Quebec Citadel.

Canadian forces (Europe) are located in the Black Forest region of southern West Germany as part of Canada's commitment to NATO. The forces consist of a land group and an air group, and are quite separate from the Canadian contingents assigned to UN peace-keeping operations.

THE POST OFFICE

In 1775 Benjamin Franklin tried to persuade Quebec to join in the American Revolution, but failed. It was not the first time he had travelled north. As deputy postmaster-general for all the British colonies, he had visited Quebec City in 1763 and established Canada's first post office.

On the same trip Franklin set up two more post offices, in Trois Rivières and Montreal. He also organized a regular mail sailing from Montreal to New York, connecting with the mail packets that sailed to Britain. The American Revolution disrupted the arrangement, but after 1784 regular European mails sailed from Halifax.

As settlers spread to Upper Canada, so did the postal service. Sleighs, stagecoaches, wagons, riders, and foot

Five days a week, an army of letter carriers speeds mail to destinations all over the country. Canada's first letter carrier delivery was made in Montreal in 1874.

carriers delivered the mail to its destinations. The whole service operated as a branch of the British post office, and it was usual for the cost of postage to be paid by the recipient rather than the sender.

In Nova Scotia, a young Haligonian named Joseph Cunard was pioneering new mail routes to Boston, the West Indies, and elsewhere. At first Cunard relied on sailing vessels, but in the 1830s he switched to steam. In 1838 he won a contract to operate scheduled mail services across the Atlantic.

In 1851, the colonies of British North America were made responsible for their own post offices. Each began issuing postage stamps as certificates that postage had been paid. Among the first stamps was the Province of Canada's famous 'threepenny beaver,' the world's first pictorial design.

Soon the mail was being carried by railway, with letters sorted while on the move. With Confederation, the Dominion government set up the Canada Post Office, which soon began surcharging letters that were not prepaid. The old custom of leaving the recipient to pay for postage was grudgingly abandoned.

In 1874 Canada's first letter carrier delivery was introduced in Montreal. As the railway network spread, postal service became increasingly swift and popular. Canada's first air mail was carried in 1918, between Montreal and Toronto. However, not until the late 1930s was air mail established for all Canada.

Today, Canada Post handles more than five billion items of mail every year. To keep abreast of the huge workload, it has introduced computerized sorting techniques at key letter processing plants throughout the country. The incoming mail is divided into two categories — standardized letters and 'other objects.'

All items are supposed to carry a six-character destination code at the bottom of the address. Standardized letters are aligned on conveyor belts, and fed to scanners that translate the code as a pattern of vertical coloured bars. The bars are printed on the envelope where

A postal worker stacks trays of letters ready for a scanner, which reads their postal codes and translates them into a pattern of coloured bars.

Dollars and Cents

Long before Canada had a standard currency, fur traders bargained in beaver pelts and Grand Banks fishermen settled debts in dried codfish. French and British coinage was in circulation, and so were the coins of many other countries and 'tokens' issued by business firms and banks.

In the 1820s, the government of Nova Scotia issued its own halfpennies and pennies. New Brunswick followed suit in 1854, and in 1858 the Province of Canada began issuing one, five, ten, and twenty cent pieces. The Dominion of Canada issued its first coins in 1870.

Until 1908, all of Canada's coins were struck in Britain. Then the Royal Mint opened a branch in Ottawa, taken over by the Dominion in 1931. Since 1969 the Royal Canadian Mint has been a Crown corporation with branches in Ottawa, Hull, and since 1976, Winnipeg, where most of Canada's domestic coinage is produced.

The first paper money issued in Canada consisted of playing cards signed by the intendant of New France in 1686. In later years the administration issued promissory notes, and so did merchants, thus paving the way for the introduction of Canada's first banknotes in 1822.

In 1936 the Bank of Canada began

issuing notes, and from then on the role of private banknotes was steadily reduced. From 1944 banks were expected to redeem their own notes but could not reissue them. In 1950 each bank paid to the Bank of Canada an amount equal to the notes still unre-

A machine stamps out nickel coinage at the Royal Canadian Mint in Winnipeg.

deemed, and from then on the central bank became responsible for all paper money.

they will be recognized by the sorting machines.

Any items carrying an indistinct code or no code at all must be processed by hand, which wastes time. They follow the coded letters to the sorting machine, which handles up to 20 000 items an hour. 'Other objects' — small parcels and odd-shaped packets that will be delivered by letter carriers — are hand-processed too.

Items travelling a long distance may be sorted several times before their journey's end. The final step comes when the letter carrier organizes his letters and 'other objects' according to his or her route, and delivers them to the door or postbox. Large parcels are delivered by truck.

Automatic sorting machines read the codes on standard envelopes and direct them to their proper destinations.

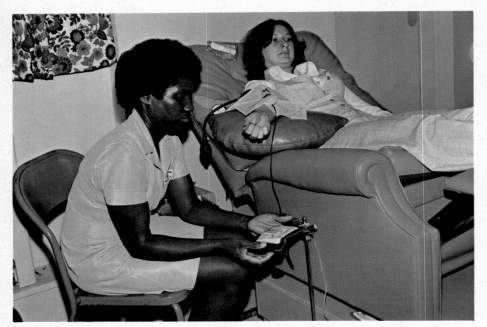

HEALTH AND WEALTH

Most Canadians take their health and prosperity for granted, but there are times when things go wrong. When that happens they can expect assistance from their governments, which provide a wide range of services promoting health and well-being.

The prime responsibility for health care in Canada rests with the provinces. They license medical and paramedical personnel, they fund hospitals, and they undertake public health programs including sanitary inspections and care of patients suffering from infectious diseases or mental illness.

Voluntary donations of blood help to keep Canada's health care system functioning efficiently.

Schools and Universities

Newfoundland's public schools are organized in 11 grades, Alberta's in 12, Ontario's in 13. The Fathers of Confederation made education a provincial responsibility, so today Canada has 12 distinct education systems — one for each province, and one apiece for the territories, not counting the federal schools on Indian reserves.

The provincial and territorial governments provide funds, set basic curricula, certify teachers, and inspect schools. Otherwise most of the responsibility is delegated to elected or appointed school boards. Their trustees erect and maintain buildings, hire teachers, prepare budgets, and perhaps decide on courses too.

Arrangements differ widely, but the typical Canadian student progresses from kindergarten towards college or university entrance by way of elementary school, junior high, and high school. However, Prince Edward Island and New Brunswick have no kindergartens, and Quebec, Saskatchewan, and Newfoundland have no junior high.

Complicating the picture even more, most provinces make special provision for linguistic and religious minorities. There are French-medium schools in Ontario, New Brunswick, and elsewhere, and English schools in Quebec (though enrolment is restricted). In most provinces religious minorities, Catholic or Protestant, are served by separate school boards.

High schools tend to differentiate between academic courses leading to university and vocational courses leading to careers or career-oriented colleges and institutes. Again, each province decides its own policies and precise arrangements differ. The aim is to give students a wide range of alternatives.

Quebec offers CEGEPs (*Collèges d'Enseignement Général et Professionel*), Ontario has CAATs (Colleges of Arts and Technology), British Columbia has special institutes covering all the province and local community colleges serving regions. They and their equivalents in other provinces give students a flying start in their careers.

Ontario and Quebec hold many of Canada's most famous universities. Among them are Laval in Quebec City, McGill in Montreal, Queen's in Kingston, and the University of Toronto. There are more than 60 other universities in Canada, some small or medium-sized, but a few of them enormous, like the Universities of Manitoba, Alberta, and British Columbia.

The campus of the University of Alberta in Edmonton, located on the south bank of the North Saskatchewan river opposite Edmonton's business district.

Federal personnel staff hospitals and nursing stations on Indian reservations and throughout the north.

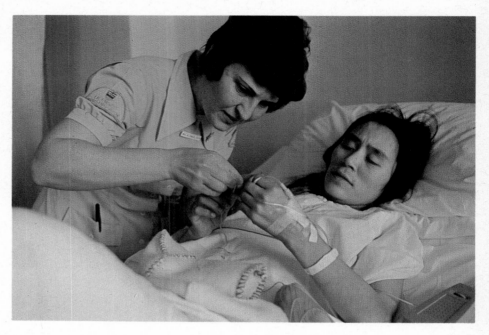

Most of Canada's hospitals are independent corporations governed by boards of trustees. Before 1947 hospital patients were expected to pay for the treatment they received, according to their means. Then Saskatchewan introduced a form of universal hospital insurance that meant patients were treated free of charge.

Other provinces prepared to follow Saskatchewan's example. In 1958 the federal government joined in, offering to provide 50 per cent of the cost of provincial hospital insurance programs subject to certain conditions. Not only the provinces but also the two territories soon took advantage of the offer.

In 1966 Saskatchewan proposed a new insurance program, this time covering the fees paid to medical practitioners. Medicare proved as popular as hospital insurance, and again the other governments wanted to follow Saskatchewan's example. In 1972 the federal government offered to bear half the cost.

Today, all provinces and territories have versions of hospital insurance and medicare, but their precise arrangements differ. In some, patients must pay premiums and user fees, whereas in others the insurance scheme is paid for out of general revenue. Some permit participating doctors to bill their patients more than the rates insured.

Unfortunately, the 1970s saw dramatic increases in the costs of health care across the country. The federal government announced cutbacks in its contributions, and the provinces had to find ways to economize. A popular technique was to treat patients at home if at all possible, thus reducing the demand for hospital beds.

The federal and provincial governments share responsibility for income security and social assistance. The federal Department of National Health and Welfare administers programs like the Canada Pension Plan and Old Age

Life expectancy in Canada extends well beyond retirement age, and senior citizens take up new interests to fill their leisure hours.

Security. Provinces and municipalities administer social assistance and welfare for people in need.

The Canada Pension Plan and its equivalent, the Quebec Pension Plan, oblige members of the work force to contribute portions of their earnings. In return they and their families are protected against loss of income due to retirement, disability, or death.

Old Age Security pensions are payable to anyone aged 65 or over who has lived in Canada for ten consecutive years, including the year preceding the approval of the application. They are also payable to anyone aged 65 or over who has lived in Canada for 40 years since age 18.

On top of the basic pension, OAS pensioners who have no other source of income are paid a supplement, and partial supplements may be paid to those with other incomes. Family allowances are paid on behalf of dependents aged under 18 who are resident in Canada and are maintained by Canadian residents.

Social assistance for the needy is provided under the Canadian Assistance Plan, funded jointly by the federal and provincial governments. The need is assessed through a review of applicants' resources, and the assistance takes the form of allowances covering items of basic need, like food, shelter, and clothing.

RELIGION

Catholics in Quebec, Mormons in Alberta, Jews in Winnipeg, Sikhs in Vancouver — Canadians place high value on their religious freedom. Churches of a dozen denominations are seen across the land, and with them synagogues, temples, and not a few mosques and meeting halls.

More than 46 per cent of Canadians are at least nominal Roman Catholics, making them by far the largest religious group in the country. They include Italian Canadians, Irish Canadians, Polish Canadians, Portuguese Canadians, German Canadians, and above all, French Canadians, whether in Quebec or elsewhere.

In Quebec, the church was deeply affected by the 'quiet revolution' of the 1960s. The provincial government forced it to surrender its traditional control of hospitals and schools, and in the cities, church attendance declined rapidly as congregations rebelled and stayed away. There was an echo of the revolution in Acadia too.

The church was forced to reappraise its role in society. Where it used to dominate, now it serves, and its bishops and priests are more flexible in their viewpoint. Like other denominations, the Roman Catholics responded to the conservative religious revival of the 1970s and their churches are full again.

Nationally, the Roman Catholic church is organized in four regional 'conferences' (Atlantic, Quebec, Ontario, and Western Canada). Each conference contains one or more archdioceses headed by archbishops, which each hold a number of dioceses headed by bishops. The bishops oversee the many individual parishes in their dioceses.

Canada's second largest denomination is the United Church, which includes roughly 17 per cent of the population. The denomination was formed in 1925 following years of negotiation among three separate denominations. Some congregations opted out, but the church came to include all of Canada's Methodists, nearly all the Congregationalists, and two-thirds of the Presbyterians.

Today, the United Church is organized in 12 conferences across Canada. Each conference consists of several presbyteries, which in turn contain a number of congregations. At each level the clergy and laity share responsibility for governing the affairs of the church, and ministers are ordained by their conference.

The Anglican Church of Canada contains roughly 12 per cent of the population, and is headed by the Anglican primate of Canada. The church is organized in four 'provinces' (Canada, Ontario, Rupert's Land, and British Columbia), each ruled by a metropolitan archbishop and further divided into dioceses governed by bishops.

The dioceses contain one or more archdeaconries headed by archdeacons, and these are divided into regional deaneries that hold a number of parishes. At every level there are elections. Parish priests elect their regional deans, laity and clergy together elect their bishops, and bishops elect their metropolitans and the primate.

The Anglican church has a long history in Canada. It was introduced to Newfoundland in 1700 and to Nova Scotia in 1710. United Empire Loyalists arriving in the 1780s increased its strength, and Anglican missionaries did much to carry Christianity to Canada's arctic.

Presbyterians outside the United Church amount to about four per cent of Canada's population, and are especially strong in Ontario. Baptists (three per cent) are mostly in the Maritimes. The first Lutherans (three per cent) came

The Anglican cathedral in St. John's, Newfoundland, is a fine example of ecclesiastical Gothic. The church was begun in 1847.

Some of Canada's most handsome churches are on Prince Edward Island, like this red sandstone building in Souris.

from Germany and settled in Nova Scotia in the 1740s.

A number of religious groups have adopted Canada after fleeing persecution in other lands. Among them have been Mennonites from the Ukraine, most of them in Manitoba; Doukhobors from Russia, who have settled in Saskatchewan and B.C.; and Hutterites, who have founded colonies in Alberta, Saskatchewan, and Manitoba.

Ukrainians immigrating to Canada between 1880 and 1914 introduced two new denominations to large areas of the west — the Ukrainian Catholic and Ukrainian Greek Orthodox churches. Ukrainian Catholics are in communion with Roman Catholics, but their priests may marry, whereas Roman Catholic priests may not.

Both Catholic and Orthodox Ukrainian congregations built distinctive Byzantine churches that are today a familiar sight all over the prairies. They

The St. Joseph Oratory is one of several outstanding Roman Catholic churches in Montreal. Pilgrims flock to the oratory to see the heart of 'Brother André,' remembered for his selfless service to the people of the city.

are easily distinguished by the crosses on their domes — standard on Catholic churches, patriarchal (three-barred) on Orthodox churches.

Canada's only Mormon temple is at Cardston, Alberta; the Salvation Army and the Pentecostal church show conspicuous strength in Newfoundland; charismatic congregations without outside affiliations have sprung up all over the country. Christianity is more diverse

than politics, and much more complex.

Of course, many Canadians are not Christian. There are orthodox and reform Jewish communities across Canada, particularly in Montreal, Toronto, and Winnipeg. There are Buddhists in Vancouver, Ismaili Moslems in Edmonton, Hindus in Toronto, and to add yet more diversity, many Canadian Indians keep alive the beliefs of their ancestors.

ARTS AND LETTERS

An American journalist was talking to the artist A. Y. Jackson about a showing of Canadian paintings. He said he expected British taste but detected none, and instead noticed French and American influence and something he could not place. Jackson suggested: 'Perhaps it is something Canadian.'

The seeds of distinctively Canadian art forms were sown early in the nineteenth century. Cornelius Krieghoff arrived in Canada from the United States and painted the scenes of habitant life that have made his name famous. His contemporary, Paul Kane, painted memorable studies of Canada's Indians of the plains and the Pacific coast too.

Several outstanding Canadian painters were active late in the nineteenth century. One was Robert Harris of Prince Edward Island, best known for his painting of the Fathers of Confederation (1883). Another was James William Morrice of Montreal, a landscape colourist who even today is the Canadian painter best known to the world at large.

Landscape was to become a Canadian specialty through the work of Tom Thomson, tragically drowned in 1917, and the Group of Seven, Toronto artists who exhibited together after World War I. Members of the group, which included A. Y. Jackson, Lawren Harris, J. E. H. MacDonald, and Arthur Lismer, influenced a whole generation of their contemporaries.

The Group of Seven disbanded in 1932. Its members helped to found the Canadian Group of Painters, which aimed to promote the arts from coast to coast. Among the members were Emily Carr of Victoria, the most eminent female painter that Canada has produced, and the water colourist David Milne of Toronto.

The noted Québécois impressionist Alfred Pellan exhibited with the Canadian Group, and remained aloof from a Montreal school of the 1940s known as *Les Peintures Automatistes*. The school was politically motivated, and among its members were Jean-Paul Riopelle, Leon Bellefleur, Fernand Leduc, and Paul-Emile Borduas.

Several new schools emerged during the 1950s. One was *Les Plasticiens* of Montreal, painting to strict geometric concepts popular in New York. In Toronto there was Painters Eleven, a group of abstract expressionists that included Harold Towne, Jack Bush, William Ronald, and Jock MacDonald from Vancouver.

In the Atlantic region, there was a school of realists at Mount Allison University in New Brunswick, much influenced by Alex Colville. In Saskatchewan, the Regina Five, including Ronald Bloore and Kenneth Lochhead, exhibited together until the 1960s. In the

Emily Carr's *Sunlight in the Forest*, **painted in about 1912.**

Northwest Territories, Inuit artists were shown how to make prints.

Today, Canadian painters command high prices at home, though few but the Inuit artists have had consistent success outside. Norval Morrisseau of northern Ontario has put Indian painting on the map, and David Blackwood and Christopher Pratt have done the same for the art of Newfoundland. Jack Shadbolt of Vancouver has been a major influence in British Columbia.

Canada has produced three notable traditions of sculpture. One is located on the Pacific coast, as represented by the totem poles of the Haidas and other tribes. The second is the stone and bone carving of the Inuit. The third is the religious wood carving of the Québécois.

In literature, no such schools can be detected. Several early classics were produced in Canada — for instance, Thomas Chandler Haliburton's *The Clockmaker*, Louis Hémon's *Maria*

Chapdelaine, and Lucy Maud Montgomery's *Anne of Green Gables* — but most of Canada's best books have been written since World War II.

Several of English Canada's finest writers have been from Nova Scotia — the novelists Hugh MacLennan, Ernest Buckler, and Thomas Raddall among them. Stephen Leacock and Mazo de la Roche were from Ontario, the province that produced Robertson Davies, Morley Callaghan, Hugh Garner, and Alice Munro.

Margaret Laurence, probably English Canada's most popular novelist, is from Manitoba. W. O. Mitchell and Rudy Wiebe are from Saskatchewan, though both now live in Alberta. Mordecai Richler and Leonard Cohen are Montrealers.

Two of French Canada's most accomplished writers are from outside Quebec — Gabrielle Roy from Manitoba and Antonine Maillet from New Brunswick. Anne Hébert and Marie-

Port-au-Percil **(1953), a landscape by Jean-Paul Lemieux of Quebec, whose large body of work has had profound influence on younger painters.**

Claire Blais are authentic Québécois, and so are Yves Thériault, Rejean Ducharme, Suzanne Paradis, and the playwright Michel Tremblay.

Pierre Berton and Farley Mowat are Canada's most popular non-fiction writers, and Donald Creighton is the best-known historian. Legions of poets follow in the footsteps of Robert Service of the Yukon and E. J. Pratt of Newfoundland, among them Margaret Atwood, Milton Acorn, Irving Layton, and Earle Birney.

Many of Canada's writers and their publishers have come to depend on the Canada Council, a funding agency set up by the federal government in 1957. Each year the Canada Council spends millions of dollars to help creators give substance to their dreams and make it available to their countrymen.

THE PERFORMERS

Theatre New Brunswick, the Royal Winnipeg Ballet, Vancouver Opera, the Montreal Symphony — thanks in part to generous government subsidies, the performing arts are flourishing all across Canada. Audiences are enthusiastic, standards have been rising, and the Canadian lifestyle has been dramatically enhanced.

Take opera, the most extravagant of the peforming arts. Vancouver, Calgary, Edmonton, and Winnipeg all have semi-professional companies that present annual seasons. Toronto has the Canadian Opera Company, built around a hard core of full-time professionals who take its productions all over Canada and to the United States.

Certainly in Western Canada, opera is becoming as popular as it is in Europe. Perhaps that is the influence of first-generation Canadians who have introduced the tastes of their homelands. The same factor helps to explain the success of choirs, chamber music, and not least, Canadian symphony orchestras.

The most famous orchestra in Canada is the Toronto Symphony, one of the most prominent in North America. The orchestra is a league of nations,

as its musicians are drawn from all over the globe. The same is true of Canada's other professional orchestras, from the Victoria Symphony to the Atlantic Symphony based in Halifax.

In many cases, musicians from the orchestras combine to form smaller chamber orchestras or chamber groups. Toronto's Canadian Brass and One Third Ninth, a piano trio from Calgary, are among the best known. Accomplished choirs include Toronto's Festival Singers and Vancouver's Chamber Choir.

For some years dance has been the fastest growing of the performing arts. Canada has three well-known ballet companies — the Royal Winnipeg Ballet, Les Grand Ballets Canadiens of Montreal, and the National Ballet of Canada, which is based in Toronto. All are full-time and each tours other parts of the world.

Modern dance troupes are smaller and less stable than the professional ballet companies, but several have made their mark. Entre Six and Groupe de la Place Royale from Montreal, Winnipeg's Contemporary Dancers, Regina Modern Dance Works — such troupes have become familiar as they tour small centres in all parts of Canada, even north of the 60th parallel.

Each summer, Dawson City's *Gaslight Follies* **recreates the kind of entertainment enjoyed by stampeders of the Klondike gold rush.**

Modern dance has much in common with theatre, the strongest of the performing arts. All Canada's major cities have professional theatre companies, but the twin capitals of Canadian theatre are Toronto and Montreal. There, the many rival companies pit the traditional against the avant garde.

Outside Ontario and Quebec, there is much interest in the work of the 'regional' theatres — professional companies that offer a series of productions through the winter months. Vancouver Playhouse, Edmonton's Citadel, Winnipeg's Manitoba Theatre Centre, and Halifax's Neptune Theatre are all front runners.

In summer, the spotlight shifts from the cities to theatre festivals in the countryside. Two of Ontario's have become world famous — the Stratford Shakespearean Festival and the Shaw Festival at Niagara-on-the-Lake. The Charlottetown Festival of Canadian musicals is one of Prince Edward Island's leading tourist attractions.

Many of Canada's professional actors have benefited from the dramatic expansion of the country's film industry.

Tax concessions make Canadian productions attractive to investors, and during the 1970s a growing number of big budget movies were filmed in Canada with largely Canadian casts.

Many of the directors and technicians in Canada's film industry were originally trained by the National Film Board of Canada (NFB). In 1939 the federal government set up the NFB to present a Canadian view of the world, and it quickly established its reputation by making documentaries and animated films that changed the face of the film industry.

Down-home fiddling is a famous art in Atlantic Canada, as here on the south shore of Nova Scotia.

Star Billing

The Academy Award for best actress was instituted in 1928. In the three following years it went to Canadians — Mary Pickford in 1929, Norma Shearer in 1930, Marie Dressler in 1931. The actresses were international stars whose features and mannerisms were familiar to millions in countries all over the world.

Since the 1930s, other Canadians have become equally famous. Walter Pidgeon from New Brunswick was one of Hollywood's leading men in the 1940s. In the 1960s, Lorne Green became everyone's idea of an American rancher through his role in television's *Bonanza*. Today it is the turn of Christopher Plummer, Geneviève Bujold, and Donald Sutherland.

Canadian voices have become famous too. Anne Murray from Nova Scotia and Gordon Lightfoot of Toronto have made their reputations without leaving Canada. Paul Anka, Joni Mitchell, Leonard Cohen, Neil Young, Burton Cummings, and many others became stars in the United States and thus the world.

Gilles Vigneault of Quebec led a phalanx of French-singing *chansonniers* into Europe. The *chansonniers'* songs reflect the special aspirations of the Québécois, and singers like

Pauline Julien, Robert Charlebois, and Claude Léveillée have already earned special places in their people's history.

At least three Canadians are known world-wide for their piano playing, though their styles are very different. Glenn Gould is one of the world's finest interpreters of J. S. Bach, Oscar Peterson from Hamilton is a jazz performer, and André Gagnon of Montreal is a light composer as

well as a performer.

Maureen Forrester, the contralto; Karen Kain, the ballet dancer; Toller Cranston, the skater; Guy Lombardo, the band leader — there has been a long list of Canadian stars. For Canadians themselves, the long-term favourites are monologists — Yvon Deschamps in Quebec, Charlie Farquharson (alias Don Harron) in the rest of the country.

Karen Kain and Frank Augustyn, principal dancers of the National Ballet of Canada, take a standing ovation at the National Arts Centre in Ottawa.

TEAM SPORTS

Remarkably, three of the world's premier team sports originated in Canada. Two of them, hockey and lacrosse, evolved as games played for fun until they were taken more seriously and became sports. The third, basketball, was invented.

The man behind basketball was James Naismith, from Almonte in eastern Ontario. As a boy, Naismith and his friends played a primitive version of basketball, aiming at peach baskets. Naismith refined the game while at McGill University, and later introduced it to the YMCA in Springfield, Massachusetts.

Appropriately, the most successful basketball team ever was Canadian, Edmonton's Commercial Graduates. Between 1915 and 1940, the all-female Grads took on every challenge yet won 502 out of 522 games — 27 of them demonstration matches at four successive Olympic Games, where they were unbeaten.

Hockey, too, came into being in Canada, perhaps in Montreal, perhaps in Kingston, Ontario, perhaps in Dartmouth, Nova Scotia. All three

centres have their supporters, but it is clear that the game had its strongest boost when Montreal students devised the McGill rules. Soon, club teams were playing against each other in leagues.

In 1893 Lord Stanley, Canada's governor-general, donated his famous cup as a trophy for the hockey champions of Canada. Competition became so keen that teams began paying imported players, and the Stanley Cup went professional. In 1909 Sir Montagu Allan presented a new cup specifically for amateurs.

Today, the Stanley Cup is the property of the National Hockey League, which contains professional teams all over North America. Among them are the Montreal Canadiens, Toronto Maple Leafs, and Vancouver Canucks, and in 1979 the league agreed to admit the Quebec Nordiques, Edmonton Oilers, and Winnipeg Jets.

Both in Canada and the United States, NHL teams consist almost entirely of Canadians, so the Stanley Cup is not awarded in vain. Apart from current heroes whose memory may dim, some players stand as greatest of the great. Among them are Howie Morenz, King Clancy, Maurice Richard, Gordie Howe,

Jean Béliveau, and Bobby Orr.

McGill University played a key role in developing both basketball and hockey, but is more famous for its contribution to yet another prime sport. In 1874 the Harvard University soccer team challenged McGill's rugby football team to play two games of football, one under each set of rules.

The Harvard men were new to rugby, and were entranced by it. Soon they introduced it to other universities, and the new game eclipsed soccer. Both American and Canadian universities developed a brand of football far removed from its British origins, introducing new rules as they thought appropriate.

In 1909 another governor-general, Earl Grey, donated a cup for amateur competition in Canadian football. As with the Stanley Cup, before long the amateurs were being unseated by professionals. Today the cup is in the hands of the Canadian Football League, which includes five franchises in Western Canada and four in the east.

Winnipeg Blue Bombers crouch on the scrimmage line. The team plays in the western conference of the Canadian Football League.

The National Game

Early settlers of New France watched Indians playing a game they called 'baggataway,' in which teams of up to 200 struggled for possession of a ball. Each player carried a webbed stick that the French named *la crosse* because it looked like a bishop's crozier.

By the mid-nineteenth century, white men were playing 'la crosse' too, introducing new rules to the game and reducing the number of players. On Canada's birthday, July 1, 1867, a team from the Six Nations Indian reserve near Brantford challenged the Toronto champions and won the game three goals to none.

One of the first acts of the new Dominion parliament was to pass a resolution naming lacrosse as Canada's national game. At the time, it was played in the open air by teams of 12. Since 1932, the old game has been superseded by six-man box lacrosse, often played in a hockey arena.

Long since, lacrosse lost its pre-eminence to upstart newcomers like hockey, football, and baseball. Even so, senior and junior teams still compete for trophies with long histories.

Lacrosse is not as popular as it was in the nineteenth century, but it remains Canada's national game.

The Mann Cup for senior teams was first presented in 1910, and annual series are held in Ontario and British Columbia alternately.

Canadian football players thrive in college teams, which take their annual championship as seriously as the professionals take the Grey Cup. At school level, however, many regions are abandoning football in favour of soccer, a less dangerous sport that supports professional franchises like the Vancouver Whitecaps of the North American Soccer League.

A fourth major professional team sport followed in Canada is baseball, as represented by the Montreal Expos of the National League and the Toronto Blue Jays of the American League. Both teams consist almost exclusively of Americans, as do the football teams — more than adequate compensation for the Canadians who play in American hockey teams.

Most supporters of professional franchises realize they have more to do with business than with sport, but that does not make them less entertaining. Their players are mentioned daily in the newspapers, their successes and failures are analyzed to the last detail, and they are rewarded by passionate local loyalties.

Curling rinks, rowing crews, and water polo teams have their successes too, but they are not as glamorous and their glory soon fades. Such teams have to rely on their own enthusiasm for a sport to make it worthwhile. That makes them *amateurs* in the true sense of the word, for they are playing for the love of the game.

B.C. takes on Ontario in a women's basketball match at the Canada Games. The sport originated in Canada.

Canada Games

Every two years, Canada holds a games of its own for teams of athletes from all the provinces and both the territories. First held in Quebec City in 1967, the games alternate between winter and summer programs that include as many sports as practical.

The stated aim of the Canada Games is 'to provide a national development competition of high calibre for a maximum number of athletes from the provinces and territories.' In other words, the point of the games is not so much victory as participation, and they prepare athletes for more important competitions.

One significant factor in games rules is the exclusion of members of

Downhill skiing is a feature event of winter programs at the Canada Games, as here in Brandon in 1979.

Canada's national teams. That means up-and-coming athletes have more of a chance to prove their worth. Besides, it helps smaller provinces to make a better showing when they confront the likes of Ontario and Quebec.

The territories send full teams to the Canada Games, but fare much better in an event of their own, the Arctic Winter Games. Held every two years, the games include not only 'western' sports, but also traditional 'northern' sports favoured by Inuit and Indians. The Canadians share the games with their neighbours from Alaska.

THE CHAMPIONS

In 1893 the men of Zorra, Ontario, became tug-o'-war champions of the world. In 1932 Emil St. Goddard of The Pas, Manitoba, won the Olympic gold medal for dog sledding. At the close of the 1970s, Helen Vanderburg of Calgary reigned as world and Pan American champion of synchronized swimming.

At one time or another, Canadians have been world or Olympic champions of sports from sailing to speed-skating and from soccer to clay-pigeon shooting. They have ranged from Tommy Burns, world heavyweight boxing champion between 1906 and 1908, to the Canadian hockey teams that were Olympic champions in 1924, 1928, 1932, 1948, and 1952.

The first world champion produced by Canada was also one of the greatest. Ned Hanlan was a sculler at a time when rowing was the world's leading sport. He honed his skills on Toronto Bay, and turned professional in 1876. In 1880 he was matched against Edward Trickett, an Australian, for the first world championship of sculling.

The race took place on the Thames river in Britain. Hanlan was not averse to gamesmanship, and played with the Australian while scoring an easy victory. He retained his championship until 1884, and by the time he retired he had won 150 races. A statue to him was erected on the shore of Lake Ontario.

Canada's second world champion was a weightlifter, Louis Cyr of Montreal. In the 1890s Cyr travelled North America and Europe, demonstrating feats of strength and offering large sums to anyone who could surpass them. Nobody ever did. In 1896 Cyr defeated a Swedish lifter in Chicago to become the world champion.

The first Canadian to win an Olympic championship was representing the United States in the Paris Olympics of 1900. George Orton of Toronto was invited to join the Americans while studying at the University of Pennsylvania, where he captained track and field. In Paris, Orton had little difficulty in capturing the 2500 km steeplechase.

Graham Smith (left) squeaks in ahead of a rival for one of six gold medals he won for Canada at the 1978 Commonwealth Games in Edmonton.

At the St. Louis Olympics of 1904, a number of Canadians entered as individuals and came home with four championships. One was for lacrosse and one for soccer. The others went to a Montreal policeman, Etienne Desmarteau, for the hammer throw, and to George Lyon of Toronto for golf.

Since the early years, Canada has steadily strengthened its presence at the Olympics, in spite of increasing competition. The first Canadian to win a track event was Bill Sherring of Hamilton, who triumphed in the marathon at the Athens Olympics of 1906. Another Hamiltonian, Bobby Kerr, won the 200 metres in the London Olympics of 1908.

At Stockholm in 1912, George Hodgson of Montreal won Canada's first Olympic golds for swimming, in the 400 metres and 1500 metres. At the Amsterdam Olympics in 1928, Percy Williams of Vancouver won the 100-metre and 200-metre sprints, the first athlete to achieve the double in 16 years.

The first Canadian woman to win an Olympic gold medal was Ethel Catherwood of Saskatoon in the high jump, also at the Amsterdam Olympics. From the 1920s, winter Olympics were held separately from the summer games. In 1948 Barbara Ann Scott of Ottawa won the women's figure skating in St. Moritz.

University of British Columbia crews in rowing events (Melbourne, 1956 and Tokyo, 1964), Ann Heggtveit (Squaw Valley, 1960) and Nancy Greene (Grenoble, 1968) in skiing, the equestrian team in the three-day event (Mexico City, 1968) — Canada's long list of Olympic champions made it all the more disappointing when there were none at the Montreal Olympics of 1976.

Of course, the Olympics are not the whole story. Canadians have done well at the Pan American Games and the Commonwealth Games, each held once in four years, and in the world championships organized for particular sports. Besides, they have triumphed in quite

separate events like marathon swims and prestige golf tournaments.

Sandy Somerville of London, Ontario, was arguably the finest golfer Canada has produced. He won the American Amateur in 1932, a far greater achievement then than it would be today. At least two Canadians have won the Boston marathon — Tom Longboat in 1907 and Jerome Drayton 70 years later.

Often competitors are eclipsed by the events they are taking part in. One of Canada's most glamorous events is the Ontario Jockey Club's Queen's Plate, first held in 1859 and the senior flat race on the continent. Even that seems young compared with the six-oared rowing race in St. John's, Newfoundland. It has been held every year since 1826 and is the oldest sporting event in North America.

PARADISE PRESERVED

Across Canada, substantial areas of land have been set aside to preserve their natural beauty and protect their wildlife. Many are national parks, many more are provincial or municipal parks, and the remainder are game sanctuaries out of bounds to the public at large.

The national parks system had its start in 1885, when Canada's government set aside 28 km² of wilderness around sulphur springs near the site of Banff in Alberta's Rocky mountains. The 'national reserve' was to be protected 'from sale, or settlement, or squatting,' and was soon enlarged to 670 km².

Meanwhile, several more 'national reserves' were created in the Rockies. Yoho and Glacier in British Columbia were set aside in 1886; Waterton Lakes, Alberta, in 1895; Jasper, Alberta, in 1907. The first eastern reserve, St. Lawrence Islands, was created in 1904. Each time the objective was to preserve outstanding beauty on behalf of all Canadians.

The first national parks created to protect wildlife were Elk Island, Alberta (1913), for the sake of elk, moose, and bison; and Point Pelee, Ontario (1918), for its bird life. The largest national park of all, Wood Buffalo straddling the 60th parallel, was set aside in 1922 to protect bison of the woods and the plains.

Today, there are nearly 30 national parks in Canada. They range from Pacific Rim (1970) on the west coast of Vancouver Island to Auyuittuq, 'the land that does not melt,' (1972) on northern Baffin Island; from Kejimkujik (1968) in Nova Scotia to Kluane (1972) on the Yukon's border with Alaska.

Some parks in the system, like Prince Edward Island (1937) and Riding Mountain in Manitoba (1929), were set aside to serve recreational needs. Others have been conserved as wilderness areas, for instance Nahanni (1972) in the Northwest Territories and Cape Breton Highlands (1937) in Nova Scotia.

Parks Canada, the federal authority that administers the system, has designated 48 'natural regions' across Canada

Helmcken Falls in Wells Grey provincial park, British Columbia. The Murtle river plunges 135 m over a lava-layered precipice.

(nine of them under water) and aims to establish at least one national park in each. As yet, only a small number of the regions are provided for, though one (the Rockies) is represented by seven separate parks.

Some parks that tourists believe are part of the national system really belong to provinces. One example is Mount Robson provincial park in British Columbia, and others are Ontario's Algonquin Park and Quebec's enormous Parc des Laurentides (1895) and Parc de la Vérendrye (1939).

Like national parks, some provincial parks are designed for recreation and some for wilderness seekers. Ontario's Polar Bear provincial park on James Bay is accessible only by air, but Manitoba's Grand Beach on Lake Winnipeg is one of the province's favourite playgrounds.

Taken together, Canada's national parks cover an area of 130 000 km². The provincial parks — more than 300 of them in British Columbia alone — probably exceed that figure. Every year provincial governments open new parks to encourage their tourism industries and serve local recreational needs.

Besides the natural parks, Parks Canada and the provincial governments operate a number of historic parks designed to preserve aspects of Canada's heritage. Some are sites little disturbed since they outlived their usefulness;

some are full-scale reconstructions with costumed guides in attendance.

The national historic parks range from Province House in Charlottetown to Lower Fort Garry near Winnipeg; from Dawson City in the Yukon to Halifax Citadel in Nova Scotia. Fortress Louisbourg in Cape Breton has been partially reconstructed, and the Plains of Abraham in Quebec City have been left open as they were in Montcalm's day.

Among provincial historic sites are British Columbia's Barkerville in the Cariboo, a reconstruction of the gold

The grey sea rolls in towards the cliffs of Gros Morne National Park on Newfoundland's west coast.

rush town, and Ontario's Upper Canada Village on the St. Lawrence. Fort Edmonton on the North Saskatchewan river and Fort Whoop-Up in Lethbridge, two of Canada's most successful reconstructions, are the work of Albertan service organizations.

A beaver lodge pokes from a pond in Gatineau park near Hull, a favourite playground for the people of the national capital.

HALL OF FAME

From time to time Canada produces remarkable personalities who make the world better or more exciting through their being in it. Some travel, some remain at home, but all contribute a sense of achievement in which Canadians can take pride. Here is a brief selection from many walks of life:

Max Aitken, Lord Beaverbrook (1879–1964), tycoon. Born and raised in New Brunswick, 'the Beaver' made an early fortune in Canada and went to Britain where he entered politics. During World War I he began building a newspaper empire, and in 1918 became Britain's minister of information. As a close friend of Winston Churchill, he entered the British cabinet again in World War II, holding a succession of portfolios concerned with the supply of munitions and other materials of war.

Elizabeth Arden, Canadian beautician.

Elizabeth Arden (alias Florence Nightingale Graham, 1890-1966), beautician and businesswoman. A trucker's daughter from Ontario, Arden joined forces with a young chemist to develop new skin preparations. In 1910 she opened a small salon in New York City, and her cosmetics found favour all over the world. Arden herself remained in control of her far-flung enterprises, both in a business sense and as a creative artist.

Norman Bethune (1890–1939), surgeon. In 1936 Bethune left his job near Montreal to help troops fighting in the Spanish civil war. Two years later he travelled to China and joined the communists, then fighting off Japanese invaders. As one of the few qualified doctors in an area containing 13 million

Emily Carr at home in Victoria.

people, Bethune worked hard to train both doctors and nurses and to develop mobile clinics. The Chinese still revere him as a hero of their nation.

Billy Bishop, the flying ace.

Billy Bishop (1894–1956), flying ace. Born and raised in Ontario, Bishop served in France during World War I and in 1915 joined the Royal Flying Corps. During 1917 and 1918 he was officially credited with destroying 72 enemy aircraft, among them 25 in 12 days and five on his last day at the front. Bishop was one of four Canadians included on a list of the ten most destructive airmen of the war.

Joe Boyle (1867–1923), swashbuckler. Raised in Ontario, Boyle made a fortune in the aftermath of the Yukon gold rush. In World War I he was commissioned to revitalize Russia's chaotic railroad system. In the process he met Queen Marie of Rumania, and assisted her in saving Rumania's treasury and crown jewels. After the war he remained her constant companion and helped to develop Rumania's rich oilfields.

Emily Carr (1871–1945), painter. After studying in Europe, Carr returned to her native British Columbia to paint the rain forests and the civilization of the Indians. She is now counted among Canada's greatest artists, but her work was ignored by the public until late in life she wrote an autobiography and other books. Through her books the public became familiar with her paintings.

G. A. Farini (alias William Hunt, 1838–1929), showman. Raised in Ontario, Farini adopted his stage name in 1860 to match and better the tightrope-walking feats of the Great Blondin above the Niagara river. He turned professional showman, and among many inventions devised the 'fired-from-a-cannon' circus trick. In the 1880s he visited the Kalahari desert in Southern Africa and reported finding a 'lost city' that has eluded explorers ever since.

J. K. Galbraith (born 1908), economist. Yet another Ontarian, Galbraith followed an academic career until recruited to head the United States' Office of Economic Security Policy, which regulated the economies of Germany and Japan after World War II. Galbraith is a long-term adviser of Democratic presidential candidates, and from 1961 to 1963 served as the United States ambassador to India.

Grey Owl (alias A. S. Belaney, 1888–1938), conservationist. In origin an Englishman, Grey Owl immigrated to

Canada in 1906 and for the rest of his life posed as a 'halfbreed' born in Mexico. He adopted Indian ways and lived by trapping, until in the 1920s he and his wife adopted two orphaned beaver kits. Grey Owl turned conservationist, and his books and lecture tours of Europe and the United States had profound influence.

Yousuf Karsh (born 1908), photographer. Karsh grew up in the Middle East and immigrated to Canada in 1925. He studied photography, and in 1932 opened his own studio in Ottawa. With patronage from Mackenzie King, 'Karsh of Ottawa' developed as the world's greatest portrait photographer. Many Karsh portraits of the famous and the mighty are accepted as classics, probing behind the facial features to seek out souls and minds.

Paul Emile Cardinal Léger (born 1904), churchman. As a young priest, Léger founded a seminary in Japan, and later served as rector of a college in the Vatican. In 1950 he became archbishop of Montreal and was made a cardinal three years later. Léger's liberal views had profound influence on the church throughout the world, especially in Quebec as it underwent the 'quiet revolution' of the 1960s. Since 1967, Léger has served as a missionary among lepers in West Africa.

Grey Owl, born A. S. Belaney.

National Photography Collection C-36186
Nellie McClung, women's activist.

Nellie McClung (1873–1951), feminist. Raised in Manitoba, McClung had early success as a novelist and entered provincial politics in Manitoba and Alberta. She played a leading role in the battles to secure votes for women and their rights to sit in the House of Commons and be summoned to the Senate.

National Photography Collection C-36186

Marshall McLuhan (born 1911), educator. Born in Alberta, McLuhan pioneered new theories of mass communications that had strong influence on the development of North American media during the 1950s and 1960s. His best-known books include *The Gutenberg Galaxy* (1952), *Understanding Media* (1964), and *The Medium Is the Massage* (1967, with Q. Fiore).

Joshua Slocum (1849–1909), sea captain. Like other Nova Scotian 'bluenoses,' Slocum spent a lifetime at sea, most of it in small vessels engaged in fishing or salvage work. In 1892 he was offered the remains of an old sloop, *Spray*, and rebuilt her. Between 1895 and 1898 he sailed alone around the world, the first man to accomplish the feat.

Vilhjalmur Stefansson (1879–1962), arctic explorer. Born in Manitoba and educated in the United States, Stefansson took part in three expeditions to Canada's arctic between 1906 and 1918. Besides discovering new land and mapping long sections of the coast, he demonstrated that white men could live off the land for unlimited periods just as the Inuit did, and had no need to transport their supplies from the south.

William Stephenson (born 1896), secret agent. Born in Manitoba, Stephenson fought against Germany in World War I. Later he travelled widely in the course of

National Photography Collection
Arctic explorer Vilhajalmur Stefansson.

his business, observed Germany's war preparations, and reported them to the British government. In 1940 Winston Churchill appointed him director of British security co-ordination in the western hemisphere, with headquarters in New York. As 'Intrepid,' Stephenson masterminded many successful secret missions that helped the allies to win the war.

John Williamson (1907–1957), geologist. Originally from Quebec, in 1933 Williamson was hired to prospect for diamonds in the African bush. In 1935 he quit the job and for five years prospected by himself in Tanganyika, now part of Tanzania. There, in 1940, he found the world's richest diamond pipe. The Williamson mine became his private kingdom, and he developed it as a model town in which all his employees lived in comfort.

FLAGS AND ANTHEMS

For years, Canada's national flag was the British red ensign emblazoned with the Canadian coat of arms. The arms consist of a shield bearing the symbols of England, Scotland, Ireland, and France, and under them a sprig of maple leaves.

Many Canadians felt the nation needed a distinctive flag of its own. In the early 1960s, a special parliamentary committee considered more than 2000 possible designs. It eventually recommended the design familiar today — 'gules on a Canadian pale argent a maple leaf of the first,' as heralds describe it. Gules means red, argent silver or white, and pale a vertical stripe.

Also in the 1960s, parliament considered Canada's national anthem. In place of *God Save the Queen*, it favoured a song originally commissioned in 1880, *O Canada*. The song had been written by Calixa Lavallée of

Fresh from their triumphs at the 1978 Commonwealth Games in Edmonton, Canadian athletes carry the national flag on a lap of honour.

Quebec to honour an official visit by Canada's governor-general, the Marquess of Lorne.

The original words of *O Canada* were written in French by Sir Adolphe Routhier. More than 20 adaptations of the words have been published in English. The version most familiar today was written by Stanley Weir in 1908 to honour Quebec's tercentenary, and consists of three verses including this one:

O Canada! Our home and native land!
True patriot love in all thy sons command.
With glowing hearts we see thee rise,
The True North, strong and free,
And stand on guard, O Canada,
We stand on guard for thee.

O Canada, glorious and free!
We stand on guard, we stand on guard for thee.
O Canada, we stand on guard for thee!

Maple leaf flags form a victory arch as the Canadian team honours medal-winning swimmers at the Commonwealth Games.

Photograph Credits

Air Canada: p. 46 bottom; Alberta Government Service: p. 38 top, p. 42 top, p. 78 bottom; Beautiful British Columbia: p. 7 top, p. 8 top, p. 35 bottom, p. 46 top, p. 90; B.C. Dept. of Mines and Petroleum Resources: p. 33 top; B.C. Forest Service: p. 36 top, p. 44 bottom; Canada Post: p. 76 top and bottom, p. 77 bottom; Canadair: p. 37 top; Canadian Broadcasting Corp.: p. 49; Canadian Dept. of National Defence: p. 74 top and bottom, p. 75 bottom; Canadian Government Office of Tourism: (Daniel Wiener) p. 3, (Crombie McNeill) p. 6 top, (Alan Zenuk) p. 14 top, (Pat Fauque) p. 15 bottom, (David Steiner) p. 30 bottom, p. 48 bottom, (Crombie McNeill) p. 51 bottom, p. 53 top and bottom, p. 57, p. 64 bottom, p. 68 bottom, p. 80, p. 81 bottom, p. 85 top and bottom; Canadian International Development Agency: p. 72 bottom; Canadian National Railways: p. 45 bottom; Confederation Life Collection: p. 18; CP Air: p. 47 bottom; Cyprus Anvil: p. 38 bottom; De Havilland of Canada: p. 47 top; Dofasco: p. 41 top; Eastern Construction: p. 41 bottom; Environment Canada: p. 34 top; Fisheries Canada: p. 32 top: Government of Northwest Territories Dept. of Information: p. 5 bottom, p. 9 bottom; Government of the Yukon Tourism and Information Branch: p. 73 top, p. 84; Health and Welfare Canada: p. 79 top and bottom, p. 87 top and bottom, p. 88 top, p. 89 top and bottom, p. 94 top and bottom: Humphry Clinker: p. 43 top, p. 59 bottom, p. 61 bottom, p. 67 bottom, p. 69 top, p. 72 top, p. 75 top; Hydro-Quebec: p. 7 bottom; James Bay Development Corp.: p. 37 bottom; John Evans Photography: p. 66; Le Ministère du Tourisme, de la Chasse et de la Pêche de la Province du Québec: p. 8 bottom; Manitoba Archives: p. 22 bottom; Manitoba Dept. of Agriculture: p. 32 bottom; Manitoba Government Information Service: p. 40 bottom, p. 44 top; Manitoba Government Photo: p. 6 bottom, p. 10 top; Manitoba Government Tourism: p. 86; Manitoba Government Travel: p. 52; National Capital Commission: (Richter) p. 50, p. 54 top and bottom, p. 55, p. 56, p. 58, p. 59, p. 62, p. 63, p. 65, p. 67 top, p. 68 top, p. 69 bottom; National Film Board: p. 64 top; New Brunswick Information Service: p. 40 top; Noranda: p. 36 bottom; Northern Telecom: p. 48 top; Ontario Heritage Foundation: p. 82; Ontario Ministry of the Environment: p. 42 bottom; Ontario Parks Branch: p. 5 top; Parks Canada: p. 10 bottom, (R. D. Muir) p. 11 top, (Ted Grant) p. 11 bottom, p. 91 top; P.E.I. Dept. of Tourism, Parks and Conservation: p. 33 bottom, p. 81 top; Port of Vancouver: p. 43 bottom; Provincial Archives of British Columbia: p. 20 top; Royal Canadian Mint: p. 77 top; Royal Canadian Mounted Police: p. 70 top and bottom, p. 71 top and bottom; Saskatchewan Government Photo: p. 34 bottom, p. 35 top, p. 39 bottom, p. 78 top; Ontario Hydro: p. 39 top; St. Lawrence Seaway Authority: p. 45 top.

Acknowledgments

Many individuals, corporations, institutions, and government departments assisted us in gathering information and illustrations. Among them we owe special thanks to the following:

Agriculture Canada
Air Canada
Alberta Public Affairs Bureau
Anglican Church of Canada
Bank of Canada
Beautiful British Columbia
Alice Brass
CP Air
Canada Council
Canada Department of Communications
Canada Department of Consumer and Corporate Affairs
Canada Department of External Affairs
Canada Department of Finance
Canada Department of Indian Affairs and Northern Development
Canada Department of Industry, Trade and Commerce
Canada Department of Justice
Canada Department of Labour
Canada Department of Manpower and Immigration
Canada Department of National Defence
Canada Department of Revenue
Canada Department of Regional Economic Development
Canada Department of the Secretary of State
Canada Post
Canadair

Canadian Broadcasting Corporation
Canadian Federation of Agriculture
Canadian Forestry Association
Canadian Government Office of Tourism
Canadian International Development Agency
Canadian Labour Congress
Canadian National Railway
Canadian Pacific Railway
Canadian Penitentiary Service
Canadian Wildlife Service
Chief Electoral Officer
Cominco
Confederation Life Insurance Company
De Havilland Aircraft of Canada
Elizabeth Arden
Environment Canada
Fisheries Canada
Geological Survey of Canada
Gulf Oil Canada
Health and Welfare Canada
Dick and Maria Hodgson
Irvin and Diane Kroeker
Manitoba Department of Tourism
Mining Association of Canada
National Air Photo Library
National Arts Centre

National Capital Commission
National Film Board of Canada
National Gallery of Canada
National Hockey League
National Indian Brotherhood
National Museums of Canada
National Photography Collection
New Brunswick Department of Tourism
Noranda Mines
Dwight and Judy Noseworthy
Parks Canada
Penny Parsons
Public Service Commission
Public Archives Canada
Roman Catholic Church
Royal Canadian Mint
Royal Canadian Mounted Police
Jo Ann Salomons
Saskatchewan Government Information Service
John and Therese Savage
Transport Canada
Treasury Board of Canada
United Church of Canada
Christine Watson

If we have unwittingly infringed copyright in any photograph reproduced in this publication, we tender our sincere apologies and will be glad of the opportunity, upon being satisfied as to the owner's title, to pay an appropriate fee as if we had been able to obtain prior permission.

Canadian Cataloguing in Publication Data

Hocking, Anthony, 1944-
  Canada

(Canada series)

Includes index.
ISBN 0-07-082693-5

1. Canada. 2. Canada — Description and travel.
I. Series.

FC60.H63   971C   C77-001609-X
F1008.3.H63

1 2 3 4 5 6 7 8 9 10 BP 8 7 6 5 4 3 2 1 0 9

Printed and bound in Canada

Index

CANADIAN STATISTICS

	Joined Confederation	Capital	Area	Population (1976)	Ethnic Origin (% 1971)		
					British	French	Other
CANADA		Ottawa	9 976 185 km²	22 992 604	45	29	26
Newfoundland	1949	St. John's	404 519 km²	557 725	94	3	3
Prince Edward Island	1873	Charlottetown	5 657 km²	118 229	83	14	3
Nova Scotia	1867	Halifax	55 491 km²	828 571	77	10	13
New Brunswick	1867	Fredericton	74 437 km²	677 250	58	37	5
Quebec	1867	Quebec City	1 540 687 km²	6 234 445	11	79	10
Ontario	1867	Toronto	1 068 587 km²	8 264 465	59	10	31
Manitoba	1870	Winnipeg	650 090 km²	1 021 506	42	9	49
Saskatchewan	1905	Regina	651 903 km²	921 323	42	6	52
Alberta	1905	Edmonton	661 188 km²	1 838 037	47	6	47
British Columbia	1871	Victoria	948 600 km²	2 466 608	58	4	38
Yukon	—	Whitehorse	536 327 km²	21 836	49	7	56
Northwest Territories	—	Yellowknife	3 379 699 km²	42 609	25	7	68